# Advance Praise for
# *How to Be a Christian and Still Be Sane*

"If you are a mainstream Christian, you desperately need this book, although you might not be able to handle its truth. Bob's book is a necessary and life-giving alternative to the glut of judgmental, thought-robbing books on the Christian market. He takes the guilt, shame, and fear out of Christianity and gives a very powerful view of what being a Christian can mean. Having grown up in a religious cult, I shy away from endorsing books like Bob's because of their insanely unbalanced nature, but this book is different. This is a book for someone who thinks and is accustomed to having a mind of their own ... or at least hoping to regain it. If you've ever questioned the sanity of Christianity and organized religion, you must read this book."
Dave Lakhani, author of *Persuasion: The Art of Getting What You Want*

"A brisk, feisty and very appealing book ... contains a poignant understanding of suffering, especially the suffering of the poor—both the economically poor and the vast number of those who are impoverished when it comes to interior resources for coping with life. Bob speaks as one of us. The book has a lively use of Scripture which is good and jolting, actually, in that it takes us off guard and plants us suddenly in Truth."
Dr. Thomas Howard, author of *Christ the Tiger*
Chairman (ret.), Professor of English, St. John's Seminary, Boston, MA.

"This book combines psychological and spiritual wisdom that will protect you from many ills. 'The Log' chapter alone will actually change your life if you take it to heart. The book is addressed as a manifesto to Christians, but it will help any

person be wiser and happier. Bob has an amazing ability to find fantastic Bible verses, great quotations, short parables, and stories that will expand your world view. It's one of the few psychological books I've read lately that doesn't blame victims.
Dr. Kevin Hogan, internationally known public speaker and influence expert, author of *The Psychology of Persuasion*

"This book is authentic, empathetic, moving, knowledgeable, sincere, energetic, and thoughtful. It is exquisitely targeted to and for practicing Christians, and should resonate with them immensely. If this book was publicly-traded, I would invest and reap rich rewards.
Paul Upham
CEO, Wesley Associates, Pawling, New York

# HOW TO BE A CHRISTIAN AND STILL BE SANE

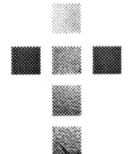

# HOW TO BE A CHRISTIAN AND STILL BE SANE

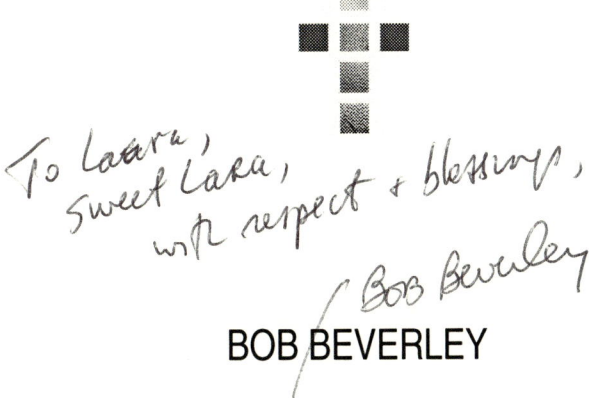

BOB BEVERLEY

iUniverse, Inc.
New York  Lincoln  Shanghai

# HOW TO BE A CHRISTIAN AND STILL BE SANE

Copyright © 2007 by Bob Beverley

All rights reserved. No part of this book may be used or reproduced by any means, graphic, electronic, or mechanical, including photocopying, recording, taping or by any information storage retrieval system without the written permission of the publisher except in the case of brief quotations embodied in critical articles and reviews.

iUniverse books may be ordered through booksellers or by contacting:

iUniverse
2021 Pine Lake Road, Suite 100
Lincoln, NE 68512
www.iuniverse.com
1-800-Authors (1-800-288-4677)

The views expressed in this work are solely those of the author and do not necessarily reflect the views of the publisher, and the publisher hereby disclaims any responsibility for them.

ISBN-13: 978-0-595-41792-6 (pbk)
ISBN-13: 978-0-595-86136-1 (ebk)
ISBN-10: 0-595-41792-2 (pbk)
ISBN-10: 0-595-86136-9 (ebk)

Printed in the United States of America

This book is dedicated to my twin brother, Jim Beverley, who has been *with me* since the beginning and has been a constant source of affirmation and love.

*Finally, brothers and sisters, whatever is true, whatever is honorable, whatever is just, whatever is pure, whatever is lovely, whatever is gracious, if there is any excellence, if there is anything worthy of praise, think about these things.*
—Philippians 4:8 (written by St. Paul from a prison cell)

# CONTENTS

Preface . . . . . . . . . . . . . . . . . . . . . . . . . . . . . . . . . . . . . . . . . . . . . . . xv
CHAPTER 1     Highway Signs. . . . . . . . . . . . . . . . . . . . . . . . . . . . . . 1
CHAPTER 2     Five Dangers . . . . . . . . . . . . . . . . . . . . . . . . . . . . . . . 5
CHAPTER 3     Get Wisdom . . . . . . . . . . . . . . . . . . . . . . . . . . . . . . 11
CHAPTER 4     The Log. . . . . . . . . . . . . . . . . . . . . . . . . . . . . . . . . . 16
CHAPTER 5     The Committee. . . . . . . . . . . . . . . . . . . . . . . . . . . . 22
CHAPTER 6     Ordinary Spirituality . . . . . . . . . . . . . . . . . . . . . . . 24
CHAPTER 7     Wake Up. . . . . . . . . . . . . . . . . . . . . . . . . . . . . . . . . 30
CHAPTER 8     Real Hell . . . . . . . . . . . . . . . . . . . . . . . . . . . . . . . . 34
CHAPTER 9     Character Rock . . . . . . . . . . . . . . . . . . . . . . . . . . . 37
CHAPTER 10    Tragedy Galore . . . . . . . . . . . . . . . . . . . . . . . . . . . 43
CHAPTER 11    Ah! Peace! . . . . . . . . . . . . . . . . . . . . . . . . . . . . . . . 48
CHAPTER 12    Mr. Dismissive . . . . . . . . . . . . . . . . . . . . . . . . . . . 54
CHAPTER 13    Everything Counts. . . . . . . . . . . . . . . . . . . . . . . . . 58
CHAPTER 14    True Magic . . . . . . . . . . . . . . . . . . . . . . . . . . . . . . 60
Conclusion . . . . . . . . . . . . . . . . . . . . . . . . . . . . . . . . . . . . . . . . . . 65
APPENDIX A    You Can't Just "Let It Go": What I've Learned from Ten Years of Being a Psychotherapist. . . . . . . . . . . . . 67
APPENDIX B    Fifty-two Additional Highway Signs . . . . . . . . . . . 73

APPENDIX C  Additional Highway Signs from Proverbs......... 81
APPENDIX D  A Love Letter............................. 85
Endnotes................................................ 91
A Bibliography of Sorts.................................. 93

# ACKNOWLEDGMENTS

I am deeply grateful to my wife, Cindy, for her integrity, goodness, and constant support. I am so thankful for my kids—Laura, Michelle, and Aaron—for they are my gems!

I am delighted by all my best friends whose love, wisdom, and varied gifts have enriched my life. So, thanks to Tom Dikens, George Colpitts, Mark Schwing, Carl and Jane Heick, Ron and Eileen Peck, Keith and Mary Beverley, Stan and Pauline McGuigan, Michael and Marcia Milea, Don and Connie Cornell, Harold and Joyce Weisel, Paul Upham, Arlin Roy, and Si and Marie Lozier.

I am also grateful for every member of my family system in Canada, the United States, and Scotland. I am proud of the Christian heritage you have passed on to me and proud of our family's integrity and decency.

I deeply appreciate the love given to me in my home church in Canada near Doug's rink! I cherish all the people connected to the first two churches I served in twenty-five years of pastoral work—the Central Baptist Church of Pawling, New York, and Netherwood Baptist Church in Salt Point, New York.

I extend my gratitude to all my teachers, ministers, therapists, and supervisors, but especially to Ralph Fogg, my first therapist, who helped me see the highway signs in my brain! Of course, I also send my love to each of my psychotherapy clients because they have taught me so much about the actual spiritual life we all live.

Thanks, especially, to Jim and Gloria Beverley, and to Andrea, Julien, and Derek for being such loving and gifted people.

Many thanks to my creative director, Gary Bielski, for his design and marketing expertise. He can be reached at gbielski7@yahoo.com. Thanks also go out to Jan Goldsworthy for her efficient and insightful editing. She can be reached at printdpg@aol.com.

# PREFACE

Christians are often portrayed as narrow-minded, guilt-inducing, and judgmental.

How accurate is this picture?

Unfortunately, many Christians think and talk in ways that lead to such a stereotype. This is a tragedy because authentic Christianity is filled with universal wisdom and on-target insights that should be displayed on highway signs everywhere.

This book is written as a manifesto to Christians to warn about the dangers that exist in our Christian mindset. My intention is to help weed out some of our blindness so that we can clearly see the beauty, wisdom, and sanity that exist within the Christian faith. It is my hope that any reader, of whatever persuasion, will be enriched by the wisdom I have found in the Christian and psychotherapeutic traditions. I also hope that this book contributes to the ongoing discussion of a healthy spirituality that is so needed in this day of sightless violence.

# CHAPTER ONE
# HIGHWAY SIGNS

As a boy growing up in Canada, I walked a mile every day in the winter to play hockey. On the way to Doug Hamilton's rink, I always noticed the big highway sign mounted on Rose Lutes' property:

*Prepare to meet thy God!*

—Amos 4:12

I was more scared of that God than of a hockey puck flying by my head at one hundred miles an hour.

I was raised in a fundamentalist church that seemed to emphasize fear over the grace of God. To my young soul, "Prepare to meet thy God" meant overwhelming fear and the anticipation of judgment.

The question in my church had always been, are you a good Christian or a bad Christian?

You knew you were on your way to becoming a good Christian if you went to Sunday school and morning worship, Sunday evening church, and Wednesday night Bible study. If you carried your Bible to church, read it every day, prayed on a daily basis, and got up to give your testimony at church when it was time for witnessing to what the Lord had done for you, you were a good Christian.

If you witnessed about the Lord outside the church to the obviously "unsaved," you reached elite status! Still, this status was pretty precarious if you slipped in any of these ways or found yourself tempted by "the world."

When I missed a Bible study class to watch the last episode of *The Fugitive*, I was sure I would go to hell. If you could have seen my insides the night I first went to an R-rated movie, you would know that the messages people teach us *really fill our souls* and shape us in profound ways. The highway signs matter.

In hindsight, I see that I grew up in what was in some ways a small and hurtful world—but it was my entire world, and its truths were certain, godly, not to be questioned, and meant to ensure my eternal well-being.

I think with great fondness of the Christians who shaped me. They loved me and cared for me. They taught me that Easter really matters and that life should be taken seriously, for it is a sacred gift. They also taught me to value discipline, honesty, and kindness.

But I have come to discover a chorus of Bible verses that I would rather have seen on that highway sign on my way to the rink. In the Psalms, King David of Israel wrote:

> *I will walk before God in the light of life.*
>
> —Psalms 56:13

All of our spiritual journeys are deeply shaped by our unique walk through life. In our frantic and fast-paced culture, it is important to know that *healthy spirituality walks*. When we walk, we are going slowly enough to notice ourselves and the people around us. When we live at a walking pace, we wound others less frequently. Our eyes can see the beauties of the world, and our ears can hear the quiet truths we need. In this way, healthy spirituality is informed by the "light of life."

The trouble with all of us is that *we live in just a slice of life*. Therefore, we do not get all the light we need. Our motto should be, "Life is like climbing Mount Everest, and we need all the help we can get."

You can allow the light in this book to profoundly help you. To assist you in that process, here's a wise highway sign from St. Paul:

> *Suffering produces endurance,*
> *endurance produces character,*
> *character produces hope.*
>
> —Romans 5:3, 4

In this book, you will read things that I call "Christian dangers" to sanity. These dangers are actually common human distortions that have a particular spin when they occur in the Christian world. Like all human beings, Christians are subject to fear, faulty programming, blindness, and a defensive posture towards anything that threatens our world.

You may already feel threatened by what I have written. You may feel that I'm about to step on the toes of your faith. I assure you that is not my intent. My purpose is to ultimately build your character as well as your faith so that you can live with more strength and hope. In short, I want you to be a sane Christian!

There are three tools that can help you as we journey along together. First, *come think with me*. I have listened to people at the depths of the human soul, and my thinking about spirituality is shaped by the truths seen from working in the raw world of human pain and struggle. So, let us reason together—with truth as our goal and thinking as our constant companion.

A second tool that can help you in this journey is *hope*. As we endure, think, and suffer, our character becomes stronger. Character is formed by endurance. If you want to get anywhere in life, you will have to endure. Acquiring and maintaining success and sanity is a step-by-step process that entails patience, perseverance, and sweat. There is no quick fix for anything that is worthy of the one life you have. The only way you can handle all that it takes to fix your life is to face it day by day, step by step. *When it comes to change and growth, endurance is always part of the process.*

Here is the beauty of endurance. It creates character, and even more beautifully, character produces hope.

How does character produce hope? In a way, it is a mysterious and complex process that happens in our souls. Let's take an area of life where people's characters are weak—let's say you are afraid to tell the truth because you are worried about what people will think of you. You then hide the truth and actually grow weaker because the fear is running your life.

Instead, you can suffer through the risk of telling the truth and find that people still love you anyway (even though it was you who stole from the petty cash!). Your character will become braver and stronger, and you will have hope because you are in the hands of a more courageous and competent self!

The pages ahead will challenge some of your thinking, question some of your actions, and display some of your attitudes in a different light. Don't despair! Your character will grow, expand, and lead you *with* hope as well as *to* hope.

A third tool that can help you is *process*. The spiritual tradition of the Bible says that there is a process of healing that is a part of our natural human condition—especially if we are looking for and working for that healing. In the world of psychotherapy, beginning therapists are told to "trust the process" that will unfold as the client walks into the office and asks for help. Clients are then told to "trust the process" when they doubt if they will ever get better. So, trust the process and yourself as you read this book, walk through its pages, focus on what is enlightening for you, and go "as fast as possible and as slow as necessary."

This book may be tough on you. If you are a Christian, it is going to show you that a great deal of what you think and feel comes from fear—not from Christ. If you are an agnostic or an atheist, you might discover that Christianity is not the end of reason. If you belong to another religion, this book may soften whatever rough edges your faith might have by illuminating our common human distortions.

# CHAPTER TWO
# FIVE DANGERS

Let's set the record straight: *Many things will hurt you and confuse you a great deal more than Christianity.* And I am not blind to the wisdom and profound truth to be found in following Christ.

Even so, we are sadly mistaken if we think that all the elements of so-called modern Christianity are healthy—and we are mistaken if we think that being a Christian protects us from emotional and mental error. St. Peter warns us in identical fashion in the following highway sign:

> *Our beloved brother Paul wrote to you according to the wisdom given him. There are some things in them hard to understand, which the ignorant and unstable twist to their own destruction, as they do the other scriptures.*
>
> —2 Peter 3:15, 16

Now this is one highway sign that radically endorses the central thesis of this book. *We are not immune from twisting and distorting even our sacred text to our own destruction.* In our ignorance and instability, we can use even our faith and our Bibles in a way that seriously harms ourselves and other people. Since this is true, I want you to think seriously with me about the following five dangers in current Christianity.

I will state each danger clearly and briefly. Subsequent chapters will expand on each of these dangers and provide a framework for a healthy emotional, physical, and mental life—which is how to have a healthy spiritual life.

**1. Honoring Theory over Real Life.** A first danger in modern Christianity is that it is often filled with way too much theory that is based on endless speculation and conjecture. Many times this theory is seen as essential to a person's life and is guaranteed to be infallibly correct. Whether it's a theory about the Second Coming of Christ, the inspiration of the Bible, abortion, homosexuality, eternal life, where to go to church, etc., the debates, talk, and discussions that surround these issues frequently miss the reality of the person doing the talking or listening.

When I was in therapy, I would often talk about a fellow Christian who annoyed me because she was very certain, argumentative, and opinionated about every theological point. One day my therapist, who happened to also be an Episcopal priest, interrupted me and loudly announced:

"She is not a Christian!"

I was stunned and said, "What do you mean?"

He replied, "Your friend loves theories. Jesus loves people."

It is so easy for us to talk incessantly about biblical inspiration and not live according to the verses that have already inspired us. It is so easy to theorize about ethical issues and fail to notice our own ethical realities. It is so easy to defend Christianity and not notice that we are hurting people's feelings at the same time—because *we are more in our heads than inside their hearts.*

St. Paul emphasizes this point in his famous chapter on love. Here's a verse that should be on every billboard in the world:

> *And if I have prophetic powers and understand all mysteries and all knowledge, and if I have all faith, so as to remove mountains, but have not love, I am nothing.*
>
> —1 Corinthians 13:2

What exacerbates the harm that can come from theory is excessive talking. The danger of so much talk is that it can serve as an evasion of action—and action is the pathway to wisdom, healing, and change. A long time ago, I read these incredible words in *The Seven Laws of Money* by Michael Phillips:

> *The human tendency to think that by saying something we have done something is so seductive that I call it elegantly evil.*[1]

Most Christians know the oft-mentioned Bible verse, "Faith without works is dead" (James 1:26). Maybe James should have also said, "*Talk and prayer* without works is dead." Let's face it: the great danger of prayer, as well as so many of our words, is that we can so easily use them as an excuse to do nothing. For instance,

I can pray for Susie in the nursing home rather than get off my duff and go visit her.

**2. Judging Others and Not Seeing Ourselves.** A second danger in contemporary Christian life is that Christians can be excessively, abruptly, and consistently judgmental. Certainly, circumstances arise when we all have to make judgments, but many Christians tend to be smug, arrogant, unkind, and ignorant when making fast and frequent judgments.

Krister Stendahl, the Dean of Harvard Divinity School, gave the Lyman Beecher Lectures on Preaching at Yale. He said something I have never forgotten:

*The commandment that Christian preachers break the most is, "Thou shalt not bear false witness against thy neighbor." And this is especially true in our preaching!*

A silence fell over the audience after he uttered that profound remark. Then he held up his hand, pointed, and said, "Especially when we talk about the Jews!"

More silence.

How much of our Christian speaking is uttered out of ignorance, stereotyping, programmed fear, and a lack of mercy and grace? Here, the whole notion of "walking" through our spiritual journey comes in handy because it takes time to know and assess others. Above all, it takes time to know ourselves—and when we take the time to look in the mirror and see the depths of our own faults, we are far more gracious to others.

The amazing thing about St. Paul, who wrote over one-third of the New Testament, is that he was constantly examining himself to see where he was on his spiritual journey. Comparing the spiritual life to a race, he says of himself:

*I do not run aimlessly, I do not box as one beating the air; but I pommel my body and subdue it, lest after preaching, I myself should be disqualified.*

—1 Corinthians 9:26, 27

**3. An Overemphasis on So-called Spirituality.** A third danger in modern Christianity is that it tends to ignore the primal reality of the body, nature, and money. Through a mistaken view of materialism and focusing extensively on so-called "spiritual" matters, there is an inherent tendency to disassociate ourselves from the earthly, financial, and natural realities of life.

We exist within the confines of our human bodies, we are bound by the physical laws of nature, and we need money to survive in society. It takes a great deal of courage, energy, and wisdom to manage our bodies, earn money, and face life head-on. When things do not go well in those departments, we always have the option of becoming super-spiritual. Then we insist that money does not matter, that a miracle will rescue us from the fate of going to the doctor, or that prayer will automatically protect us while we're driving in an ice storm.

One of the amazing things about the Bible is that it faces every aspect of life head-on. It does not avoid topics such as sex, money, illness, murder, incest, violence, the loss of animals, menstruation, aging, and death. The Bible recognizes that life is not simple. If life were simple, the Bible would be a very short book. Likewise, if life were a super-spiritual, "just trust God" affair, the Bible would only consist of a few short paragraphs.

**4. The Danger of a Christian Subculture.** As sociologists tell us, and as we all know, every group tends to be focused on itself and less shaped by outsiders. And most groups are even suspicious of the outsider. Christians can exhibit the same patterns in their suspicion that people of "the world" will seduce them away from the Lord. Christians can then live in their own subculture with their own language, music, viewpoints, and opinions. Surrounded only by Christians, the church will look like a religious gated community.

The saints in the Bible really grappled with their circumstances in the light of their faith, beliefs, and unique calling. As we think of Abraham, Moses, Ruth, Jeremiah, St. Peter, Stephen, Timothy, St. John, or Elijah, we immediately picture them as immersed in the details of their unique communities. They were all knee-deep in their local reality. The Bible is not a gated community! This is very clearly stated in the instructions that Jeremiah gave to the Israelites when they were taken away in captivity to Babylon:

> *But seek the welfare of the city where I have sent you into exile, and pray to the Lord on its behalf, for in its welfare you will find your welfare.*
>
> —Jeremiah 29:7

When reading the Gospels, in particular, you can see that whenever Jesus confronted people who were different from him, they were always amazed at how well he knew them. And they were even more amazed at how much he loved them. The Son of Man was a "friend of sinners," immersed in their reality, because he also knew that there was nowhere else to go.

Jesus knew that every human situation, institution, family, and person was an amazing combination of good and evil, shrewdness and folly, light and darkness. He taught that this tangled web—the weeds and the flowers all intertwined—cannot be fully discerned and untangled until the full light comes when he walks back into town. In this sense, ironically, there can be no gated community.

**5. Hell and the Casual Talk Surrounding It.** Christians talk calmly, easily, casually, and glibly about their neighbors' eternal destruction, but they do very little about it, and it seems they never cry about it. This is absolutely crazy! Jesus had to face the same craziness in his day.

His disciples saw that certain people were not receiving Jesus, and so they asked him, "Lord, do you want us to bid fire come down from heaven and consume them?" He turned to them and said:

> *You do not know what manner of spirit you are of: for the Son of man came not to destroy men's lives but to save them.*
>
> —Luke 9:54, 55

In summary, there are five ways in which being a Christian can do you some mental harm. We can use theory to harm and ignore ourselves and others. We can be too judgmental. We can be over-spiritual and not face the laws of nature, our bodies, and money. We can hide in our Christian subculture, and worst of all, we can consign people to hell in a callous and arrogant manner. I know there are systems of belief and lifestyles that are far more deadly. Unfortunately, these elements lead people to develop a warped Christianity that is not sane and healthy.

Now, here are my questions: How are you doing? Have you stayed with me so far? I know this can be challenging, but have you been able to handle it? You have? Good, because let me share with you a real challenge. When I told my secular friends about this book, they almost all said that Christians would not read this book! Why did they think that? They were convinced that Christians are too isolated in their subculture, unable to imagine that they have something to learn when it comes to spirituality!

If you are with me so far, you are the exception I was hoping for, and I believe you will be rewarded for being that exception. In the pages ahead, I will throw a lot at you to counter the stereotypical Christianity that thoughtful people reject. More importantly, I will show you the resources in the Christian faith that can help you become wiser, saner, and more peaceful.

This book will highlight hardly noticed Bible verses that will shine a deep, poetic, and easy-to-understand light on the darkness within our minds. I'll combine this with the images and sayings that I have created in my unique psychotherapy work to help dispel the fog of craziness that has the potential to harm us all.

In this chapter, we have started to work our way out of the fog—but there is even more light ahead.

# CHAPTER THREE
# GET WISDOM

◆

*(in which we begin to battle the five dangers)*

Sanity is the ability to see reality, face life head-on, and put things in perspective. In a sense, sanity is wisdom. With that in mind, I will share with you the first highway sign I would display on every road in the world.

*The beginning of wisdom is this:*
*Get wisdom, and whatever you get, get insight.*

—Proverbs 4:7

This thought comes from Solomon, King of Israel, a man considered by many to be the wisest man of ancient civilization. Even though Solomon had everything—power, fame, plenty of parties and pleasure, and even more money, he advocated that every one of us get one thing above all else—wisdom.

Wisdom is what we must find as we battle the crazy-making falsehoods of contemporary Christianity. You may feel overwhelmed by all that we have dealt with in the previous chapter. I hope that you saw a great deal of truth in what I pointed out. If so, we can look for more wisdom to help us offset the irrelevant theories and distortions that can hurt us.

I want you to "get wisdom" in relation to the five dangers that can hurt our spiritual lives. This may not be as hard as you think. It isn't just a matter of finding wisdom. It is also a matter of recognizing the wisdom we already possess and guarding it as a priceless treasure. For example, if what I said in the previous chapter struck home to you, then you have already gathered some wisdom in relation to these issues.

To follow Jesus is to humbly get wisdom and to question ourselves every now and then. In this regard, here's another highway sign for your sanity:

> *The wisdom from above is, first of all pure, then peaceful, gentle, open to reason, full of mercy and good fruits without uncertainty or insincerity.*
>
> —James 3:16

There, my friend, is the biblical mandate to *think*. We are called to be "open to reason." Here is the biblical dismissal of all narrow-mindedness, ignorance, and stupidity. If you agree even slightly with me that there are real dangers in current Christian circles, then we are commanded to set aside our uncomfortable feelings and reason together.

We need to reason together because we are all quite blind. We are blinded by many different things—custom, habit, and fear, to name but a few. We are also blinded by familiarity as our brains become so accustomed to our worlds that we no longer see them with fresh vision.

I want to tell you the number one explanation why we are all blind. Here is a concept I learned in psychotherapy school that will help you better understand why people are so messed up.

Take anything in your life that is what the Bible calls sin or what psychotherapists might call pathology. The trouble with the sin or the pathology is that it becomes *egosyntonic* to you, meaning that the pathology is so much a part of you that you are one with it—*and you don't even notice it.*

The purpose of therapy or sanctification is to make the sin or pathology *egodystonic* so that there is a dissonance between your ego and the pathology.

We are all, in one way or another, in one pea soup of a fog—and we don't even know it. The reason we don't know it is that we have become the fog. With wisdom's help the fog lifts. So, a very greedy person wakes up to his or her lack of compassion and is astonished at his or her former blindness to the needs of others.

I have a client who is a New York City firefighter. One night in therapy, I told him of an idea I had that every person should put into practice. I proposed this idea rather casually, and to tell the truth, I didn't give it much thought. At our next session, this man told me that my idea was one of the best ideas he had ever heard. It is something we will call the "Committee." It is the best way to fight our egosyntonic pathology. It is an idea so practical, so powerful, and so intuitively correct that I guarantee it as the best tool against our blindness.

I invite you to select a group of people from your life. It could include your spouse, your minister or rabbi, a business colleague, and a few friends. They should be people who are firm and gentle. The job of this Committee is to meet every few months to assess and evaluate your life based on the goals, dreams, and standards that you have articulated for yourself.

We must realize that coaches, friends, and critics are, as the British Parliament says, "the loyal opposition" when they point out something that we don't see. We need prophets and alarm clocks to wake us up.

So, then, let's spruce it up a bit. You should have people on the Committee who are strong in areas where you are weak. Seek out people who have a somewhat different outlook on life than you because

> ... *in a variety of counselors, there is safety.*
>
> —Proverbs 11:14

Above all, they should be able to hold your feet to the fire.

If you understand the impact this idea could have, you'll realize that it could change your life. You should also feel scared. You will be opening yourself up to a clear field of accountability and feedback. This idea is very scary indeed!

But listen: What happens normally is far scarier. Normally, when people in your life see how you are screwing up, they talk about you behind your back and wonder when you are going to wake up to such things as:

- Your weight gain
- The way you speak to your spouse
- How tired you are looking
- The foolish things you say when you are nervous

In case you are too scared to implement the Committee idea, here are two sanity-producing questions for you:

1. Do you have *anybody* in your life who can speak the truth to you in love? You could at least have a one-person committee!

2. How good are you at listening to your own personal feedback? Do you listen to that quiet voice inside you that is whispering, "This isn't working"?

There is an old saying that goes, "If one person calls you a horse, ignore him. If two people call you a horse, start thinking about it. If three people call you a horse, buy a saddle." This idea was simply stated by Jesus in one of his frequent expressions:

*He who has ears to hear, let him hear.*

—Mark 4:9

But if all our viewpoints are viewed as infallible, there isn't even an option of looking for feedback. By battling our blindness, we begin to battle all our dangers, especially harmful allegiance to our theories. When we honor our theories over real life and real people, we don't see what is going on in front of us. We cannot test ourselves, be open to reason, and have ears that are open to further truth as the Bible calls us to do.

A central path to sanity and happiness is to live in reality and see what is going on. To do this, you must think—and thinking is a communal effort. Minds are sharpened by other minds. If all minds think the same, there is no benefit. We stretch and grow through differences.

Thinking wisely is at the heart of sanity, healthy spirituality, and Christian living. Thinking wisely and living wisely are the alternatives to theories that are irrelevant, insensitive, and unloving. Wisdom is the biblical alternative to foolishness and ignorance. As Ernest Homes said, "Ignorance stays with us until the day of enlightenment, until our vision toward the Spirit broadens and casts out the image of a no-longer-useful littleness."[2]

Christianity should actually lead people to be bigger. Christ emphasized gratitude, reverence for all people, compassion, thinking outside the box, and seeking eye-opening wisdom. None of this makes people small and petty. Christianity is a way of life that seriously calls us away from a "no-longer-useful littleness."

Wisdom is the biblical alternative to human smallness, and the beginning of wisdom is *get wisdom*! In this regard, I want you to look at one verse from the New Testament where Jesus talks about what corrupts us. As I've already said, he knew that the biggest source of corruption is located within:

> *It is what comes out of a person that defiles. For it is from within, from the human heart, that evil intentions come: fornication, theft, murder, adultery, greed, wickedness, deceit, envy, slander, pride, and …*
>
> —Mark 7:21–22

Lo and behold, the final thing Jesus says that also corrupts us—an item that also appears in this parade of defilement—is one that really surprised me:

*Foolishness*

Wow! It is amazing to see the company that foolishness keeps. The reason I'm emphasizing "foolishness" here is that in our foolishness, we do not see how harmful it is. In the next chapter, I will share with you the number one easy, ordinary, commonplace way in which we are foolish.

To get ready for it, I want you to leave your house, go into the woods, pick up a two- or three-foot log, and bring it back into your home. I'm serious about this. Go get the log. It could change your life.

# CHAPTER FOUR
# THE LOG

◆

*(in which we battle the second danger, judging others and not seeing ourselves)*

I hope you went into the woods and got your own personal log, because what you can learn from that log can change your life. In fact, I am tempted to tell you that this one combination of thinking and acting is the key to changing the ways in which Christians are perceived and received everywhere.

How are Christians perceived and received? In general, Christians are often perceived as judgmental people who are quick to condemn, **quick to exclude**, and apparently suffer no guilt or remorse as they gather their wagons in a circle and talk about all the "lost" outside the circle. Of course, this perception is a generality and a stereotype—and there are always exceptions to any stereotype. In my experience, however, there is enough truth in the general perception of Christians to do something about it!

This is why you and I need to pick up a log, hold it, and then meditate on the following teaching from Jesus:

> *Judge not, that you be not judged. For with what judgment you judge, you shall be judged. How come you can see the speck in your brother's eye, and can't see the log in your own eye? First, take the log out of your own eye and then you will see clearly to take the speck out of your brother's eye.*
>
> —Matthew 7:1–5

Are you still holding the log? If you are not, or if you didn't even go get the log, well, thanks for being honest, and welcome to the club.

What is the club? It is the club of people who read self-help books and do not do the exercises. If you didn't go get the log, let me tell you that doing so will display one of the best "object lessons" you'll ever receive along the path to sanity.

So … go find the log, pick it up, and read the verses by Jesus. I did this exercise myself while I preached on this text, and by picking up the log and holding it during my sermon, I was able to see the central truth in this verse that I had never seen before.

Yes, I had already seen the truth in the statement that as soon as we judge others, we are in for this 99 percent guaranteed response—we will get judged back. Tell your wife she didn't do something, and chances are, in a New York second, you will be told what you have not done.

Yes, I had already seen the truth in the concept that you must first clean up your own act before you can helpfully assess others. It's hard for people to take you seriously when you have a log in your eye! By the way, notice I did not say that we couldn't, at times, accurately assess others with logs in our eyes. An alcoholic can accurately tell us not to drink so much. The issue is that we usually resent advice that is so freely given and not first applied to the person who gives it!

In picking up the log, I was able to see, in a powerful way, that Jesus is telling us something like this:

> *For God's sake, and for your sake alone, you've got a four-foot log in your eye. You'd better do nothing else other than get to the hospital and remove the log!*

In other words, he's saying something like this:

- You're having a heart attack, and you're sitting there telling your friend that he doesn't drink enough water.
- You have no money in the bank, your bank has called, and you are about to bounce six checks unless you get there by 10:00 AM—and you're sitting there telling your brother he spent too much on dinner last night.
- You are 200 pounds overweight and about four weeks away from obesity-related cancer, but you are spending all your waking moments trying to get your husband to stop cluttering the kitchen counter (and he spends all his time trying to get your kids to chew gum with their mouths closed).

You see, this is the great advantage of knowing other people. If you're married, if you have children, or if you work with other people, you can spend 90 percent of your time looking at other people's faults, and then you do not have to wrestle with your own log!

He or she who has ears to hear, listen: This is the easiest way to be crazy and insane—to walk around noticing the splinter in your brother's eye and doing nothing about the four-foot log sticking out of your own head.

He or she who has ears to hear, listen: If you want to radically improve your life, spend virtually all your time working on your own logs. Notice I said *logs*, because just when you get one log out of your eye, after a while you'll notice there's another log stuck in there that must be removed.

*Life is a never-ending log-removal project.* Once you realize this fact, you will become more gracious, humble, and merciful. Take a look at your own log and you'll lose some of the arrogance and self-righteousness that plagues so many of us Christians.

It is truly a tragedy that Christians are known to be so judgmental and critical. We are commanded to be different by our own sacred Scripture. Read the following highway signs:

> *Therefore let anyone who thinks that he stands take heed lest he fall.*
> —1 Corinthians 10:12

> *Brethren, if a man is overtaken in any trespass, you who are spiritual should restore him in a spirit of gentleness. Look to yourself lest you also be tempted.*
> —Galatians 6:1

This would be an ideal time for you to notice the small, quiet voice inside you that may be pointing out the log in your eye. Why? Because you've got a log in your eye! And *now* is the time to deal with it—because you've got a log in your eye!

We have Jesus to thank for the wonderful, disturbing image of the log. We can imagine that walking around with logs in our eyes damages our chances of getting through to people—and keeping the judgmental logs in our eyes kills our chances of growth. All in all, the logs make us look rather foolish.

We all come by our foolishness in an unsuspecting way. It's so easy for us to see other people's faults. We know we've had a few, but we become complacent. We are in a hurry. We focus on tomorrow. If someone points out our log, we are more stung by their remarks than by the truth of their remarks. Thus, we really never notice our own logs, let alone work on them!

In fact, something worse happens.

In our foolish state, not only do we not see the logs in our own eyes, we actually think of the logs as beauty marks. For example, our drunkenness becomes a badge of honor, our lust is a sign of freedom, our anger is celebrated as our independence, our convictions become signs of our commitment, and our bitchiness is viewed as our prophetic talent.

In this respect, our foolishness creates and shapes our self-understanding. Phillip Brooks, a wise nineteenth-century Boston preacher, wrote about the process of sin as moving from initial fear of the sin and the horror of committing it to actually doing it with trepidation and guilt. Then, once we do it, we do it a second time, and then it becomes easier to do it the third time. We then become proud of our sin and boast about it, and then finally, we put down those who do not do it.

Does this sound familiar?

Time also plays a part in this common folly.

Imagine that you have just started to grow a log in your eye today. For example, let's say it is a Sunday night and you have just successfully blown your first paycheck over the weekend. A beloved uncle who has been visiting you for the weekend couldn't help but notice your spending spree and he asks to have a chat.

He puts his arm around you and says, "I used to live like this with my money for the first ten years of my career, but my dad told me something when I was 32 that changed my life, and with your permission, I'd like to pass it on to you because I love you so much."

Since your log is only one weekend old, it is only the size of a splinter. Therefore, you are not too defensive, and you invite your uncle to speak. He says that his father told him to save 10 percent of everything he earned, and because he listened to his father, he is now a millionaire, although no one would suspect it, given the old jalopy he drives! Because his advice was given in love and because you were open to his feedback, you decide calmly to follow it.

Now imagine a different scenario. Imagine that you have blown every paycheck for 10 years. Imagine that same uncle wants to give you the same advice. Now you are in a much different position to hear him. The years of debt and impulsive spending have filled you with despair about your financial position. You have developed a defensive posture toward anybody with money and the advice that often goes with it. To cover up your defensiveness, you now view your log as a beautiful sign of spontaneity, freedom, and living in the moment. Now nobody can get through to you!

It takes years to see how the years affect us—but they do. Alas, sooner than we expect, we all get to see the ratcheted-up, multiplying effect that time does to any of our faults and problems. It is one thing if you are a fool for one year, but it is way different when you have been a fool for a decade. You may not get to see it in yourself, but you'll see it in others ... and vice-versa!

Here is the simple, tough truth. If you think it's bad to have a log in your eye right now, imagine having it in your eye for ten years! The trouble with having a log in your eye for ten years is that you get used to it. In fact, you get so used to it that you don't do anything about it. You don't even see it at all. You look around it, adjust to it, compensate for it, eventually glorify it, and above all, spend twenty years looking at your neighbor's log and gossiping about that.

Lord, have mercy on us all.

In the meantime, you can see that our moral task as Christians is figuring out how we can keep people from becoming comfortable with their logs. But that is a task for further down the road. The question at this stage in our journey together is: How can you and I become alarmed enough to do something about the four-foot logs in our eyes?

Here is my foolproof, partly rare, guaranteed three-step process to alarmingly, actively taking the logs out of your own eyes.

- **Step 1:** Call the Committee and tell its members what you think your log might be. See if they agree with your assessment.
- **Step 2:** Brainstorm the specific ideas, tools, and actions that can pluck the dead wood out of your life.

- **Step 3:** (This is the rare part.) For one year, promise yourself that you will not dispense advice or criticism to anyone. (Hey, I know this isn't a Bible quote, but this idea should be up on a billboard in Times Square!) In other words, you are out of the speck-finding business.

All right, I know how crazy Step 3 sounds. So, yes, if people specifically ask for your advice and discernment, we will grant you permission to speak. And, yes, if you are raising children, you are allowed to tell them not to play in traffic. And, yes, if your friend thinks it's a garden snake and you know it's a poisonous copperhead, your monastic vow of critical silence can be broken—but now for God's sake, do it quickly so you can save his life and then get quickly back to saving your life by becoming that *very* rare wise person who quietly is working away at his or her own log and steadily becoming more sane.

# CHAPTER FIVE
# THE COMMITTEE

◆

*(a brief handbook for all Committee members)*

We all belong to a Committee, whether we know it or not. Each of us evaluates our relatives, friends, neighbors, and colleagues. And certainly each of us has a Committee inside our own mind that constantly holds court on us. Here is some guidance for log work:

*The first requirement for Committee members is candor.* We need to have the courage to "speak the truth in love" (Ephesians 4:25). More harm is done by silence than anything else in this world. We are afraid of what others will think of us if we speak the truth to them—and so we keep quiet as they walk in darkness. We don't want to hurt people, but we hurt them by not caring enough to speak up.

*A second requirement is sensitivity.* Although we all need critical feedback, it is misused by impatient, judgmental people. We often treat people poorly because we've had a bad day or because we are mad at how we are living. We chew out other people because we are living far from our own ideals. Or, sad to say, sometimes we give people a kick in the pants because we want to impress the world with how tough we are—"My, what a good kicker!"

In general, committee members should pay heed to the following advice: "People will not always remember what you said. They will not always remember what you did. But they will always remember how you made them feel."[3] The wisdom in this thought by Maya Angelou cannot be overstated!

A third requirement of Committee work is *patience*. Patience is needed because people are not healed overnight. We are in Committee work for the long haul.

People need lots of encouragement, affirmation, and compliments. In essence, Committee work is about love. Love is the fountain of candor, sensitivity, and patience.

# CHAPTER SIX
# ORDINARY SPIRITUALITY

◆

*(in which we battle the third danger: sentimental super-spirituality)*

The Christian world is often accused of being naïve about evil and sentimental in its clichés and slogans. In a world rocked by tsunamis, earthquakes, hurricanes, and tornadoes, it seems insane to say that God won't give us more than we can bear or that everything happens for a reason.

Let's put it plainly: The world is a tragic place. Christians should know this because no book says this as well as the Bible, and yet the Christian world is often full of "explanations" that are quite sentimental.

The central fact that should blow away all sentimental super-spirituality for Christians is that God became incarnate in a human being. The Christmas message on a highway sign is

> *And the Word became flesh and dwelt among us, full of grace and truth.*
> —John 1:14

There is hardly a trace of sentimentality in the teaching and actions of Jesus. His teaching did not minimize the evil and brokenness of the world. He wept, spit, groaned, grew tired and frustrated, and eventually bled to death. At his death, he felt forsaken by God and shouted it with great clarity and agony.

We often hear the cliché "God won't give you more than you can bear!" This, however, is not a quotation from the Bible! It even contradicts the experience of one of God's tough followers. Read this highway sign from St. Paul:

*We do not want you to be ignorant of the affliction we experienced in Asia; for we were so utterly, unbearably crushed that we despaired of life itself.*
—2 Corinthians 1:8

The Bible does not say, "Everything happens for a reason," nor does it say that we are supposed to forgive everything. There are rafts of verses in the Bible where the saints have "had it" with people. They exhibit anger, rage, disgust, dismissal, contempt, and exile. St. Paul, for example, had this to say about troublemakers:

*If a man is causing trouble in the church, go tell him that it is his fault. If he doesn't listen to you, find another person and tell him. If he still doesn't listen, bring him before the whole church. Then, if he doesn't listen, kick him out. He is worse than a tax collector and is self-condemned.*
—Titus 3:10, 11 (see also Matthew 18:15–17)

That verse is a far cry from endlessly putting up with people's non-compliant behavior and thinking that all the Bible says is to *forgive*.

The Bible is full of tearful agony, heart-wrenching awareness of evil, judgments against evil doings, and clear visions of the chaos of human life.

If you don't believe me, go read Ecclesiastes—a book so astounding in its depiction of the vanity, evil, and emptiness of life that it would amaze many people that it is actually in the Bible. Ecclesiastes is *the* scriptural response to all sentimentality and any Christian spirituality that denies the tough questions and realities of life.

Here is the most staggering verse in this regard:

*Just as the deer is caught by the hunter, and the bird is taken in a snare by the fowler, so man is caught at an evil time and*
*Time and chance happen to all.*
—Ecclesiastes 9:11, 12

The presence of this book in the Bible is the most glaring example of open-mindedness I know because this book could easily have been written by an agnostic or an atheist. In fact, if many atheists or agnostics would read Ecclesiastes, they would know that believers who do not convey the darkness of the world are not conveying the darkness in the Bible.

Romans 8, written by St. Paul, says the same thing about the tragedy of the world: "The world groans with agony and suffering as we await the coming of Christ."

In essence, the answer to the super-spirituality of our current day is the grounded spirituality of the Bible that does not ignore the plight of the poor—whether our poverty is that of character, money, time, health, or peace. In essence, every page of the Bible recognizes the massive healing that is needed for the kingdom of God to be in our souls and in our nations.

There is a consequence of understanding our obstacles: each of us must be committed to working very hard to have spiritual health. *We will not be rescued by anything other than a massive effort.* We need lots of rowing, lots of prayer, and lots of miracles. And everyone must "report for duty" (as the California preacher, E. V. Hill, used to shout in one of his sermons).

This massive effort will help offset a subtle danger in human psychology. Most human beings are prone to being passive-dependent on stronger people. In our weakness, we can rely too much on others. This tendency can be rather dangerous in us Christians when it is combined with the fact that miracles and prayer are part of our heritage.

We can develop a magical and miracle-expecting view of the world. This can make people a bit crazy because in expecting a miracle, you can miss the natural laws of life.

I remember when I was very young, my brother and I would play "catch" with one of the sponge balls that my father would bring home from work. Invariably, one of us would miss a catch, and the ball would disappear within the tall grass beside the garage or into the hay field next to our house. Being a good little Christian boy, I would pray that I would be able to find the sponge balls. Despite my many prayers, my father brought home about a hundred sponge balls every summer because that grass and hay were so thick and deep that we could never find the ones we had lost.

In short, I should have just cut the grass!

It is so easy for prayer and dependence on God to become a substitute for action or a blinder to the harsh realities of life, most of which are much tougher to deal with than lost sponge balls. In this respect, reliance on prayer or an expected miracle can lead Christians to become passive and out of touch.

I cannot tell you how prayer works and how often miracles are part of the landscape. But I do know that people will not trust us Christians if we do not see life head-on and walk in the "light of life." As St. Benedict ruled, we must "*work* and pray."

Here's a shortcut guide to healthy spirituality and sane living, along with some healthy theology, in three sentences:

- *Imagine you are out in a rowboat in a storm.*
- *Pray as if you had no oars.*
- *Row as if there is no God.*[4]

As most of us examine our lives, we all know that what is really in question is whether we are rowing! It takes courage, sweat, and determination to row. It is far easier to hide behind our various religious excuses than to admit we were scared to row and did not grab the oars! For example, if we are having financial problems, it is easier to say "the Lord will provide" than to have the courage to get a second job!

It is fatally easy to engage in endless speculation. I love the spirit and truth in the following verses:

> *The secret things belong to the Lord our God, but the things that are revealed belong to us and to our children forever.*
>
> —Deuteronomy 29:29

> *I desire that you insist on these things, so that those who believe in God may be careful to apply themselves to good deeds; these are excellent and profitable to men. But avoid stupid controversies, genealogies, dissensions and quarrels over the law, for they are unprofitable and futile.*
>
> —Titus 3:8, 9

This is the heart of spirituality—thinking and living that is helpful to people. A hundred Bible verses could be marshaled to say that the essence of spiritual health is simply whether we love God and our neighbor. The authors of the Bible would lament all the dissensions and quarrels that have been part of Christian history and are not "excellent and profitable" to people.

These verses also invite us to pay thankful attention to what we know and not waste our time with the secrets. The secrets belong to God. How much time do we waste quarreling about secrets and mysteries and the unexplainable? In this sense, the Bible does not endorse long-winded theoretical discourse. Instead, it invites us to see and manage ourselves with love—and to also love our neighbor. The value that lies within this process is that you are listening to your soul and paying attention to where you are needed.

In this sense, healthy spirituality is a lot simpler than we think. I know someone can write five hundred pages of theory about all kinds of spiritual topics. For example, you can write volumes in an attempt to figure out what constitutes God's voice inside the individual and what is actually one's own voice. At the very least, what it means to be spiritual is simply to pay attention to your experience, your intuition, your heart, and the lump in your throat. Pay more attention and you might notice the following:

- I'm really nasty to others when I'm tired. That's not fair.
- I should visit my aunt in the nursing home.
- I hate war and I'm going to march in the anti-war rally.
- The jabbing talk at the office really hurts and I've got to do something about it.

*Being spiritual means paying attention to the major and minor revelations that occur in your life.* It means paying attention to the complexity within you. In short, you are not just a body, a machine, or a vessel that some dictator tells what to notice. You are a unique author of your own spirituality. Yes, God is at work within you, but you have to notice what dreams and callings and truths are catching fire within you.

Being spiritual means comprehending what is before you! This is the more positive flip side of log work. As we remove logs from our life, we can capture the flow of insights and actions. These actions and insights are close to us and within the unique river of our own spiritual waters.

I have listened to a great many people in my day. People walk into my office with a hunger to be heard. In being heard, they are then able to hear what is going on within themselves and eventually see more of what is going on around them.

I think this kind of simple attention to our own experience is at the heart of a much-needed and healthy spirituality. This is why I distrust so much lengthy spiritual talk about obscure things. I distrust lengthy talk about angels, demons, the afterlife, the Second Coming of Christ, etc. I distrust even lengthy talk about the Bible because I think the authors of the Bible would want us to get back to ourselves as their words shine light upon us and the needs of our neighbor.

# CHAPTER SEVEN
# WAKE UP

✦

*(in which we battle the fourth danger, Christian subculture)*

The world is a very beautiful place. It is filled with many kind and talented people as well as all the loveliness of nature, art, music, and a thousand other delights. But the world is also a tough place—filled with too many dangerous, critical people who are disagreeable in a thousand ways. The world is saturated with powerful institutions that can crush people in a heartbeat. And there are viewpoints and beliefs and attitudes that poison us so slowly and subtly that we don't even notice it.

So, it is very tempting and understandable for any group to want to live in its own small world and keep the big, dangerous world at bay. Christians will want to be protected and fortified by the light that is found in worship, sermons, praying, studying the Bible, talking with other Christians, reading sound theology books, and walking in wisdom—but this does not mean we are to disappear into a Christian subculture.

There are three reasons why doing so presents a major problem: First is the fact that the world needs followers of Jesus. Jesus called his followers the "salt of the earth" and "the light of the world." Christians are people who make a serious attempt to be loving, thoughtful, grateful, and kind. The cry of the prophets is that the essence of religion is not obscure thinking or ostentatious worship. No, it is:

> *Render true judgments, show kindness and mercy each to his brother, do not oppress the widow, the fatherless, the sojourner or the poor.*
> —Zechariah 7:9

> *The Lord has showed you, O man, what is good;*
> *And what does the Lord require of you*
> *But to do justice, and to love kindness,*
> *And to walk humbly with your God?*
> —Micah 6:8

If you are a Christian, your neighbor needs you. A paralyzed veteran needs a visitor to assuage his loneliness. The business world needs people of integrity. The justice system needs lawyers who return phone calls. Hospitals need more nurses. The world needs as much salt and light in it as all the good people can muster.

This brings us to a second reason why we are not to disappear into a Christian subculture. Notice that I wrote "all the good people" in the above paragraph. *Christians are not the only people who are just, kind, and charitable.* There are all kinds of people who do far more good for the world than we can imagine. If Christians remain in a subculture and do not really know their neighbor, then we run the risk of "bearing false witness against our neighbor" and therefore miss all the good people who are more on our side than we comprehend.

For example, we would rather be operated on by a competent surgeon who is an agnostic, than a Christian who is an incompetent surgeon. A competent surgeon (of whatever persuasion) is very much on our side, and we should honor their God-given talent, skill, and common humanity.

The third reason why Christians are not called to live in a Christian subculture is the example of Christ. Jesus did not live in the religious subculture of his day. He was *in the world* and saw, understood, and loved its people. Jesus could see how harassed and helpless people were, like sheep without a shepherd. He could see the tremendous forces that work against people. His ministry to people was one of lifting their burdens, not burdening them with a theological load that would break their already burdened backs!

Here is my favorite little-known description of Jesus:

*A bruised reed He will not break*
*A flickering candle He will not quench.*

—Matthew 12:20

That prophecy from Isaiah about the Messiah accurately describes the tender, compassionate, and sensitive aspect of Jesus.

Jesus knew people. He could see a "bruised reed" of a person and treat him or her gently. He could see someone's "flickering candle of faith" and fan it into more life. He didn't blow out people's faith by yelling at them for not having perfect faith.

Jesus knew people had short attention spans, so he gave short parables. He knew people were defensive, so his clever twists maneuvered with pinpoint accuracy to the people in front of him. He knew people would forget things, so he offered stunning picture images. He knew when to be tender and when to be tough. Jesus had such amazing ability with people because he was *with* them.

This point is crucial because the central spiritual reality of the Bible, apart from God, is people. The central revelation of the Bible—what is always revealed right in front of us—is our neighbor who needs us. There is much that we do not know even if we walk in the light. But we can always love our neighbor.

This chapter is a serious attempt to grab you by the arm and simply say, *"The world needs you! Don't worry so much about what you cannot explain or understand. Spend your time and energy doing something about what you already do know."* This is the hallmark of sanity, the hallmark of following Christ. Christ saw what was in front of him—people who needed his help. He gave them that help in a unique, specific way because he saw the thoughts and actions they specifically needed. Jesus did not live in a Christian subculture. He had a loving commitment to the world.

One of the consequences of the Christian subculture is that very few churches truly honor the jobs and responsibilities that people have in so-called secular workplaces or their own homes. Churches are often experienced as the place of ministry—and faith commitment is seen in people doing more and more church work.

St. Paul faced this challenge with the Christians in Thessalonica. They were so preoccupied with the coming of Christ that they were not attending to their duties. St. Paul advised them in no uncertain terms that they were to

> *do their work in quietness and earn their own living.*
>
> —2 Thessalonians 3:12

This kind of spirituality is hard to teach and live in the American culture where fame, success, wealth, and the glamorous life are so seductive and appealing. Christians are not immune to this virus. The Christian subculture even has its various versions of the famous and the successful. In my opinion, churches at their best are places where people can be really known as individuals and invited to do their work in the world as their ministry.

For example, take Bill the plumber. He has a dirty job involving long hours, frequent emergencies, and customers who are at their wits' end because their basements are flooded. By the time Bill shows up in church on Sunday, he is tired because he has actually been a down-to-earth savior to many people. He has unclogged toilets and bathtubs, stopped floods, and helped clean up the world.

Bill's church should invite him to rest on the Sabbath. They should honor him for the noble work he has already done. If he is up to it, Bill should be asked to speak about his work because he is fighting chaos like the Creator in Genesis. To the mother with three children whose washer and dryer is working again, Bill's ministry is as important as any preacher's. In fact, if you think about it, Bill may save more marriages than any therapist because it's hard to stay in love when the toilets aren't working.

Do you know of any church that really honors Bill the plumber?

# CHAPTER EIGHT
# REAL HELL

♦

*(in which we battle the fifth danger, casual talk about hell)*

Let me clue you in on what a therapist's job is like. It is a dirty job. I hear about more evil in one week than most people hear in a year or even a lifetime. I know that people can be wicked beyond belief, and they can display a selfishness that is absolutely breathtaking.

I have done long-term work with pedophiles, incest victims, trained elite soldiers, drug dealers, and prostitutes, among others, and I make this promise to anyone who is scared to tell me something: after you tell me whatever you are embarrassed to tell me, within twenty seconds I will tell you a story I've already heard in the same area that is far worse.

I have *nearly* heard it all, so please understand that I am well aware of the effects of evil and do not underestimate its poison and power. The victims of evil visit me every week. Therefore, I know there is room for judgment in healthy spirituality. There is room for judgment in Christianity—on earth and in heaven.

In my work I see the lifelong consequences of evil. Therefore, in my view, only heaven can make up for the miseries of this world. In my opinion, agnostics should be more tempted by the idea of heaven on behalf of the victims of the world.

Heaven and hell is Jesus' way of taking evil seriously. He was so serious about evil and hell that he was willing to go to hell for us.

Nevertheless, the way in which modern Christians talk about hell is the *craziest* talk I hear in any given year—bar none. Christians talk so glibly and casually about Hell. You will recall here that this, in my view, is the biggest turnoff and danger in Christianity. *Is there a bigger ethical disaster than Christians who talk easily about their neighbor going to hell and do nothing about it?*

Jesus wept for the victims of evil. That is a far cry from the casual conversations and dry-eyed sermons where the "unsaved" are put in their place. I have sat many times with people and heard them tell me something like, "Jack died last night. Too bad he wasn't saved," as they kept eating their salad. Neither their hearts missed a beat nor their mouths a bite of food.

As a Christian alternative to this insensitive insanity, let me point you to what I consider to be the two greatest moments of love in relation to evil. The first is St. Paul's, revealed in Romans 9, where speaking of the salvation of Jewish people, he said, "For I could wish that I myself were accursed and cut off from Christ for the sake of my brethren, my kinsmen by race." He was willing to trade his salvation for theirs. That's a far cry from calmly assigning others to hell while doing nothing about it!

The second great moment of love in relation to evil is Jesus saying from the cross, "Father, forgive them, they know not what they do!" I consider that grace the only hope for us all.

Yes, there is immense evil and misery in this world, but if we do not weep about that tragedy and do something about it, we are in our own hell of blindness and coldness, which does not do justice to the spirit of Jesus. And, as C. S. Lewis said, "the door to hell is locked from the inside."[5]

Hmm ... the door to hell is locked from the inside. That may give us a clue to a healthier alternative to the casual heartlessness that surrounds almost every discussion I've ever heard about hell.

Perhaps we can distinguish doctrinal hell from real hell. Doctrinal hell is an almost always insane theoretical discussion that abstractly and academically consigns people to hell because they do not fit in our categories. Real hell is the hell people put themselves in and throw away the key.

Real hell is where Jesus met people—on earth and in his descent to hell between Good Friday and Easter. Picture Jesus meeting the rich young ruler on earth or into hell. In either place, he would not be merely a category to Jesus. And Jesus would not put him in hell because he is a Jew or a Muslim or a man or a Pharisee or a liberal or a conservative.

Jesus would see that the man has put himself in hell through his greed and self-isolation. He drinks like a fish and is being consumed by cocaine. He is becoming smaller than he can imagine. Jesus would have compassion on him. He would show him amazing grace. And Jesus would shine some light on the guy. After all, the light that shows us we are messed up is also the light that heals us.

# CHAPTER NINE
# CHARACTER ROCK

◆

*(an explanation of why we are the way we are)*

We have to be strong people to endure the hell we are in and to fight evil in ourselves and others. However, it is very hard to be strong and loving because of the way we are as human beings. To understand this, let me share with you my *Island Theory of People*.

Picture one of the islands of the world, such as Australia, Haiti, or the Bahamas. Of these three island nations, it is clear that Australia is stronger in terms of money, population, geographic size, resources, and unity of government. The Bahamas is weaker than Australia, but it is far stronger than Haiti, which is one of the poorest and most divided countries in the world.

If you compare yourself to any of these islands, which one would you feel most like inside yourself? Is your inner world big, strong, and unified like Australia? Or is it fragmented and broken like Haiti? Or is it like the Bahamas—a group of smaller islands that aren't quite as together as Australia but nevertheless get along better than Haiti?

Notice how easy it is to see the world of countries. It is far harder to see the insides of people. It would be absurd for us to expect that Haiti is going to be a big force in world charity or that the Bahamas can defeat the United States in a war. Yet we are often asked to do the absurd and the impossible when it comes to our characters.

For instance, people are often asked to "let go" of a terrible hurt. We are sometimes admonished not to let something get to us. The truth is the exact opposite. Never in your life have you *let* something get to you! Either things get to you or they don't. When they get to you, they hurt so much that it is impossible to let go of them as if you were dropping a snowball.

"Let it go" and "don't let it get to you" are said by people who cannot see your inside and do not have empathy for your inner reality.

Imagine a team of men and women at a sales meeting. The boss comes in and rips everybody apart for a bad month of sales. Every person in that room feels a tear inside his or her soul, or at least a nick of pain, as their jobs are threatened. The males, however, would be automatically trained to hide their pain with jokes, all the while saying that the women are being "too sensitive."

Aren't there some people who would naturally be less hurt at the sales meeting? Yes, and this is where the island theory comes in. Some people are more like Australia, and as a result, their response would come out of a stronger character that is unified in self-confidence and power. In short, some people have developed more internal muscle than others—and that internal muscle is character.

An easy way to understand this way of looking at people is to think about boxing. Have you ever wondered how boxers can withstand the punishment they endure? Here's how to find the answer: Go carefully up to a boxer and feel his leg, chest, stomach, and arm muscles. They will feel like they are made of rock! The boxer has trained his body and soul to withstand punches.

Likewise, there are some people who have developed their internal muscle by building up muscles of self-confidence, self-delight, and a quick, well-defined response to attack. How can we become that sort of person? Well, the answer would necessitate a book in itself—but the place to start would be to recognize the need to become that sort of person. If we have a weak character in a certain respect, we would need to see ourselves that way and then work on becoming a stronger person in that respect.

In other words, the healing begins when we notice the actual wound that needs healing. Healing begins when we see the reality of our situation. If you read your Bible carefully, you will find that there is a constant plea for us to see the reality that people are in and to match their situations and characters with our response.

One of the great beauties of the world of psychotherapy is understanding people at a very deep level. But the purpose of therapy isn't merely to be understood. It isn't just meant to understand or empathize with someone's inner child of hurt and pain. The purpose of therapy is to strengthen the ego.

Strength, however, begins with a proper diagnosis. With that in mind, let me share with you the brief but insightful Freudian tripartite structure of our human insides.

According to Freud, our insides are basically composed of three structures. First of all, there is the *ego*, which is meant to be the CEO of the soul. If you want to lose weight, the ego is supposed to be in charge and say, "No dessert after dinner tonight."

At the same time, we have another part inside us that Freud called our *id*. The id is Freud's word for the powerful bundle of appetites we have for all kinds of pleasure—like eating a hot chocolate sundae with gobs of whipped cream. In the deepest parts of our soul, there seems to be no sense of time, so we are very much into immediate gratification. For the id, the only time is *now*.

Suppose you order the sundae one day after the ego has announced its new diet. A third factor comes into play in the deep parts of our being, which Freud called the *unconscious*. As soon as you begin to think about the sweet dessert, your *superego* shows up and starts berating you for being a lazy glutton, etc., etc. The superego is the part of us that contains our morality and our conscience.

If you know your internal landscape, it often looks like this:

**Superego**

Ego

**Id**

Your ego is jammed between two huge forces. In the Freudian view, the unique combination of your particular superego, ego, and id makes up your character. The Latin word for character comes from the word *rock*, and what that means is that our character, even if it is a so-called weak character, is set in stone. Therefore, if you are nervous, fear-filled, guilt-ridden, or ashamed of yourself, that stuff is set in you like concrete.

The deep understanding of character in psychotherapy work matches the wisdom in the Bible. Neither tradition imagines that change comes easily or quickly for human beings. A masochist is not going to change overnight any more than a 130-pound man can change into Charles Atlas after a weekend at the gym.

Likewise, if you are paranoid (very afraid), narcissistic (have a PhD. in self-centeredness), obsessive (need the world very lined-up), borderline, depressive or manic-depressive (David in the Psalms), angry, lustful, and arrogant, you will not be able to change any of that overnight either.

Countless Bible verses can back me up on this one. Jesus said that some people's homes are built on sand, and there will be trouble when the rains come. Jesus says that much of our growth is blown away, not only by the winds of life, but by our own conflicting desires.

All this can be summed up in an image of people that St. Peter used in his second Epistle. Some people, he said, are "mists driven by a storm" (2 Peter 3:17). Oh my Lord! What a perfect description of broken character! That phrase sums up what we can learn in a lifetime about people. For example, you come home at night and you are HALT—the acronym AA people use for **H**ungry, **A**ngry, **L**onely, and **T**ired. You are a mist being driven by a storm. No one is home, and that feeds your loneliness, so you unconsciously head to the computer for some cybersex. Lust, the wild storm, has kicked in, and you are even more a mist driven by a storm. Add some rum to the mix, and the storm will be further increased. Then the mist will get mistier.

If people are like this—and we all are at one time or another—you can automatically see why some self-help books, some sermons, and some pieces of advice are unhelpful. If their words do not come from an understanding of our unique brokenness, it is like throwing a brick in a puddle and expecting to build a house! You can't expect a mist to become a tidal wave. You can't expect a storm to behave.

This concept explains a teaching of Jesus that I always had trouble with. Jesus said,

> *To him who has will more be given, and to him who has not even what he has will be taken away.*
>
> —Mark 4:25

I always thought Jesus was being mean and judgmental when he said that. Now I see that he was just describing life, reality, and you and me. He was actually saying that life greases the track in the direction you are going.

If you are a mist, chances are you will stay a mist and be driven around by internal and external storms. If you have a more powerful character, chances are you will stay that way and grow stronger, which will allow you to handle the storms of life better than a "misty" person.

Does this mean there is no hope for people like you and me who may be misty? No, there is hope. If there were no hope, I would not be a psychotherapist or a minister. Still, I recognize how big the storms are and how misty we all can be.

What is the basis for realistic hope? The hope is that people can look in the mirror, pray hard, work hard, think more clearly, behave differently, and feel good about the changes they can make inside and out. The mist can become a storm of love, peace, and wisdom that can fight the storms of anger, selfishness, and destruction that hurt our lives.

So we have character like concrete and we can be mists driven by storms—and that isn't even the end of it. We also are affected by:

- The health of our bodies
- The amount of money we have
- The systems in which we exist
- Our community support

If these things are not going well, and we are overwhelmed and discouraged, often what we are being asked to do is impossible—and that is still not the end of it. There is also one more *big* thing to consider as you attempt to fix your life: do you *have the time* to implement the changes that are needed? How many times are we asked to do something for our improvement, and yet the truth is we do not have the time to do it? In my opinion, *depression is 70 percent a mixture of being overwhelmed and tired—and that is why the help offered us has to accurately assess our total life situation and the resources at our disposal, including time.*

There isn't a page of the Bible that does not recognize this description as the way life really is. Each one of us is deeply shaped and affected by our character, our health, our financial situation, and the state of our community and nation.

Because all of these things are real and powerful, there is a cry for justice, wisdom, kindness, and fairness in the prophetic voices of the Bible. The prophets know that the miracle the world needs is the daily miracle of love and healing for the oppressed.

We are invited to love others with our strong character, too—and it does take strong character to love. Character is strengthened by getting wisdom, acknowledging our blindness, working on removing our own logs, listening to our Committees, and walking in the light.

And we need that strength because we are often hurt by other people—a painful reality we will address in the next chapter.

# CHAPTER TEN
# TRAGEDY GALORE

◆

*(in which we battle the blindness of hurtful people)*

The Bible is filled with page after page of verses that record the unexplained evils of the world. It is filled with tears, rage, sorrow, and blood. In this sense, I trust the Bible much more than I do the smug explanations of psychologists who specialize in blaming victims.

If you read many self-help books or a sampling of the new age Web sites that are all over the place, you will come across thinking like this:

*There are no victims, only willing participants.*

Psychologists, marketers, and spiritual gurus often write things like this to help people see their self-defeating attitudes—but the subtle and obvious ways in which victims are blamed by our theories is staggering. Picture a rape in Central Park. Picture the fifty million killed by Hitler and Stalin during World War II. Picture Auschwitz ... and you will know that there are victims.

You can see the same thing at work in the books and Web sites that tell you not to take things personally. If we all could be this way, we wouldn't have to work to be exquisitely kind, sensitive, just, and fair because people would be able to "just let it go" or not take it personally.

If the world were as simple as our clichés, the Bible would be a very thin book. If the world matched our sentimental faith, the Bible would be a very thin book. If the world matched our blaming of the victim, the Bible would be an extremely thin book—about the width of the finger pointing at us for being such crybabies who take everything so personally!

If nothing should bother us, if it all can be wiped away by a psychological trick, then there's not much need for help. Yet, if rape really hurts the soul of a woman, if murder ravages a family with agony, if an unjust firing sends someone into economic hell, we may just need a friend or two, not to mention something far more comforting than our useless clichés. Instead, we must also get as many things working for us as we can.

In this respect, prayer helps because prayer is our way of damning evil and hoping for a better day. Through prayer, we ask for more than just a breezy psychological spin on things.

The trouble with the current psychological spin is that it impedes our sanity. How can we bear it when we are first blamed for what others have done to us and then told not to take it personally? The grain of truth in this craziness is that the explanation for people's behavior is them, not us:

- The people who said you are ugly are blinder than Ray Charles, and they are hooked to the culture-bound notion that only Pamela Anderson is pretty.
- The boss who fired you did so not because you are lazy, but because your laughter reminds him of his father's laughter—and he hates his father.
- The person who stabbed you did not do so because you were greedy in a prior life but because he had been hooked on heroin for five years and would sell his mother to slave traders for "just one hit." You just happened to be walking by the wrong corner at the wrong time.

Can anyone get to the point where they wouldn't take the point of the knife very personally? Can anybody be fired and say (without even minor pain), "It's transference"? Can you be so self-assured that if someone were to say you are ugly that it wouldn't hurt a bit?

Answer: Sometimes, but not always. Not even the person who possesses the greatest sense of maturity can keep off all hurt. (Even Jesus was hurt by others—"How long am I to bear with you?" is one of his candid remarks.) We can, however, lessen the hurt much of the time.

In fact, here's a way of looking at it that allows me to help you to never take anything personally. Take in the examples below:

- I offer you my hand in a handshake.
- I offer you a piece of cake.
- I invite you to an all expense paid cruise to Alaska.

In each case, you look at the offer, think about it, and then shake my hand, take the cake, and accept my invitation.

The act of taking is a conscious, time-invested choice. Often when we get hurt, we have no choice in the matter. You stroll into your boss's office expecting a pay raise and instead notice the two guards beside his desk carrying the empty bags meant to contain your office accoutrement.

*You're not given the time to take.* It's a blow instead of a handshake. It's a poison being shoved down your throat rather than cake being graciously offered to you. Hurt is like being in the middle of your Alaskan vacation and then being kidnapped and dragged to Haiti.

In short, you did not *take* it personally. Your soul was violated by cruelty and you had no choice but to be hurt. It is no different than a sudden, unexpected punch to the gut. Even a boxer would be hurt if he didn't have the time to tighten his stomach muscles.

Here is true essence: we all get rabbit-punched in life—and it's not our fault at all.

Here's a true story that happened to me. It changed my life, and it could also change yours.

Back in the mid-1980s, while I was in therapy school, I was easily wounded, so I would almost always stay silent when being unfairly treated. I carried quite a bit of unconscious guilt around in my soul. I was still a pastor at my first church and I had just started going to therapy.

A man named Steve started coming to my church. He was a friendly, cheerful soul who happened to be a resident at the nearby psychiatric hospital. I befriended Steve because I adored his cheerful spirit. I ended up taking him for drives, buying him lunch, going to the movies with him, and doing other special things for him. After about a year of mutual regard, on one particular beautiful Sunday, I was greeting people at the back of my church after the worship service was over. Various parishioners were saying, "Nice sermon. Have a good week," when all of a sudden, Steve bolted past everybody and ran out the door.

I caught him in the parking lot and asked him what was wrong. He said, "I'm never coming to this church again!"

I asked, "Why? What happened?"

He replied, "I'm not talking to you."

I said, "Steve, tell me what happened because we try to fix things around here."

He reiterated his position that he was not talking to me or coming back to church. I then said, "Steve, for all that I've done for you, I at least deserve an explanation."

Steve looked coldly into my eyes and said, "What did you ever do for me?"

I stood there on that beautiful blue-sky day and realized that Steve's cold, unfair comment did not cripple me. Was it because I didn't take it personally? No, it was because I did not take it at all. I knew while we were talking that his medication was slipping and that he had become crazy.

I also knew that I was innocent with regard to him—in fact, I was more than innocent. I had been very decent to him. Therefore, when he asked, "What did you ever do for me," I knew he was crazy and that I had done plenty of things for him. His comment stung for a moment, but I wasn't reeling in agony! The blow had been blocked by two groups of muscles—an awareness of the person he was at that moment and an awareness of the person I was.

While standing in that parking lot, I had a further epiphany. I'd already realized that I wasn't lying in a heap of psychic dust—and that was remarkable. But I also realized that when other people hurt me, sometimes they are more like Steve than I'd ever imagined.

None of us can come close to "taking nothing personally". But we can see where people are coming from, recognize more of our own goodness, and be centered (muscled) on that wonderful reality.

Around the same time that the Steve episode occurred, I was leading a Bible study at my church in Pawling. The text we were looking at was on a right-hand page of my Bible, and I was glancing at it just before we got started. Then my eyes moved over to the left-hand page, and I got smacked in the head and heart by the following passage in which Jesus gave his disciples advice on dealing with other people as they spread his message:

> *Go into a house and offer it your peace;*
> *if they don't want it, let your peace return to you.*
>
> —Matthew 10:13

Be a good person, offer the world your goodness, and if people don't want it, let your thermostat of internal peace be set by your good character—not by what the world does with it.

# CHAPTER ELEVEN
# AH! PEACE!

Fear is by far our most powerful emotional enemy. I am convinced that fear is what is behind the five dangers in Christianity we have examined in this book.

It is because of fear that we easily exclude those who are different. It is because of fear that we strive so hard to be the same as other Christians—because if we are like them, we will feel safe in our look-alike harbor. In my opinion, we often spin irrelevant theories, talk about extraneous things, nod in agreement to sentimental teaching, and ignore the broken realities of our bodies, wallets, and countries—because we are afraid to face the issues that make us wake up in a cold sweat.

Jesus knew this because he talked constantly about fear and anxiety, which were also predominant themes in the ministry of the beloved Pope John Paul—"fear not" was his first public proclamation as Pope.

In this chapter, I will share with you some highway signs that can help us live in more peace and less fear. The Bible contains many beautiful benedictions, many of which come at the end of St. Paul's letters. The word *benediction* comes from the Latin word for *blessing*, and the following blessing is as sublime as any when it comes to addressing our fears.

Think of your fears, guilt, and anxieties—and let the following highway sign fill you with calmness, peace, quietness, and a relaxed hope.

> *Now may the God of Peace Himself*
> *give you peace at all times in all ways.*
>
> —2 Thessalonians 3:16

This is my favorite benediction. And what a contrast to fear and guilt!

We've all sat in the chair of fear. We've all slept in the bed of doubt. We've all been paralyzed by the inaction that comes from fear. It sometimes seems like a miracle that we ever get out of that chair. That's how powerful fear can be and how it keeps us in our place.

The first thing you need to do when you are in fear is *get out of the chair*. Don't sit there anymore. Get up, take a shower, and if nothing else, go have lunch with someone. Chances are they need you as much as you need them.

As we take the first step away from the chair of fear and anxiety and then make the first step in the direction of our dreams, we see that we're still alive, and we find some success. We then develop a bit more courage and take more steps, and eventually we can become successful at battling fear.

I wish right now you could come to my offices so I could show you all my books, articles, and magazines. They are everywhere. I have books in my bedroom, hallway, den, church office, and psychotherapy office. My desk is jammed with files full of the quotes and little articles from which I have culled the best for you.

I have notes detailing the brilliant things clients have told me. I have class notes from my college, seminary, and psychotherapy training. I listen to audio tapes and CDs. Every week, I take notes from my colleagues in supervision and case conferences. I read text posted on Web sites to gather more wisdom, stories, and insights. I have hundreds of pages in my files where I used to take notes from all the fine preachers I heard while I was in college or seminary.

You get the picture. I love thought, wisdom, reflection, and insight. I didn't know it, but when I was walking by the sign on Rose Lutes' property, I was pretty empty, confused, and dozy. I was hanging on by a thread. What I have done throughout the years is what I recommend to you. I have gradually filled up my spirit with a ton of the world's wisdom. I know it has saved my life and led to much of my success.

Spirituality is the viewpoint that we should strive to fill up our spirit—just as we strive to fill our bank accounts!

But wisdom, insight, and thinking will only get you so far. Action is the indispensable companion to wisdom and peace that will take you where you want to go. St. James put it this way: "Faith without works is dead." (James 2:17) We could also say *wisdom without works is dead*. Wisdom that does not lead to action is irrelevant. Thomas Watson, the founder of IBM had the word THINK posted behind his desk. That's fine. My sign would say *Think and Act*.

Here is the foolproof way to fight fear, guilt, anxiety, and despair in your life: become a person of action. If you are sitting in your chair or lying in your bed, the worse thing to do is to keep sitting in that chair or lying in that bed trying to argue with fear, worry, guilt, or lethargy. You must get out of that chair, bed, or room and get on the move. Get out! Get going!

Here's another highway sign:

> *In all toil there is profit.*
> *Mere talk tends only to want.*

—Proverbs 14:23

When authors or speakers focus on changing your beliefs and don't get you immediately doing something different, the value of their advice is overrated. Let's think of one area where you want to improve your life. Perhaps you want to have more self-respect or confidence. You can't just look in the mirror and say, "I have more self-respect." You must live in a way that is different—that gives you more pride because you are living according to your ideals. If you want to be a better husband, you must perform the actions that show your resolve.

In my own life, I am a far more confident therapist than I am a confident golfer because I have done the things in the therapy world that lead to more confidence. I got training, gave and received feedback, saw clients, heard many clients say they appreciated my work, and then continued to add improvements to my interventions and techniques. In golf, I have never gotten any training, never entered a tournament, never fixed my terrible swing, and never received any endorsements. Mere talk and little effort won't lead to much change.

This may sound harsh, but it really isn't. What is harsh is all the emphasis in self-help books and marketing on "easy" ways to become a winner in various areas. Reality does not work that way. Success takes thought and solid belief, but more than anything, *it requires improving action after improving action after improving action*. The so-called "easy" way backfires because we can't instantly become successful by following quick fixes. In the end, it leaves us feeling more like losers, and when we feel like losers, we stop in our tracks and do not act. Then we are doubly hurt because action is the most powerful weapon against fear.

To succeed, we must be people of action in the area in which we want to succeed. Fear also stops us in our tracks and keeps us in our beds, chairs, and couches as it pushes on our backs and chests, filling us with doubt and its varied paralyzing poisons. The opposite of fear is love—and love leads us to action because "love" is a verb. As you walk in love and do loving things, your fear decreases. It will not decrease if you do nothing!

It is so bad for you to do nothing. You feel useless, and feeling useless is the one unnoticed pathology of our time. This uselessness is a direct result of the focus on fame and "elsewhere living" in our culture. If your job does not count because it isn't "in," famous, or godly, if your relatives don't count because they are not TV stars, you are going to feel pretty useless—and that won't help you fight fear.

This is where the whole notion of sacred living comes in as our helper. In this deep Christian view of life, *there are no little people and no little places because every inch of earth is sacred and everybody matters.* That's why if you get out of the chair and go visit somebody, chances are you will feel better—because you were visiting someone who is sacred.

But despite our good intentions and our actions, we are all still afraid. The best article I have ever read on fear was printed in the *New Yorker*.[6] It is called "The Cornerman," and it is about a boxing trainer named Teddy Atlas. The author emphasizes the power of fear in the boxing ring. Atlas talks about the fear held by boxers and says that he watches boxers in the ring make what he calls "the silent contract":

> *If you don't punch me too hard, I won't punch you too hard.*

We all make that "silent contract" with ourselves. Here are some examples:

- I won't hold you to too high a standard if you promise to keep the bar low enough for me.
- I will let you get away with mediocrity if you let me slide by as well, and then we'll both pretend that we're living with excellence.
- I won't tell you that you're spending time on petty things if you don't point out that I'm wasting my time, too.

We are often too afraid to punch hard at life and go for the win. If we hold back and are not accountable to ourselves, we can ignore the fact that we never gave it our all. The silent contract covers our fear of failure.

Nothing stops us from acting as abruptly as well as fear. For example, fear is telling me that I should stop writing this book because "it's all been said before and no one will buy it!" Now fear is telling me I shouldn't reveal my vulnerability. What can one say to this kind of fear?

Let me share two secrets it took me years to discover.

>I ask: What if no one likes my writing? How do I deal with that fear?

>The answer: *That's not possible! Of course, someone will like it!*

Why is that not possible? Because the seed will always bear some fruit. That is the first secret. Someone will get some benefit from this action. The good action is better than a worse action, and good actions always pay dividends.

The good actions always pay dividends because goodness is its own reward. As a friend of mine says, "It is also a matter of honor because honor lies in doing the right thing, whether accepted or rejected by another."

The second secret is that we also do good things for ourselves. We are saving our own souls, capturing our own truths. For example, I wrote this book for myself as well as for you. I offer it to you in peace, and the peace returns to me.

So far, I have put all the focus on action to help us lessen our fears. Still, *we must also notice our intentions when it comes to fear.* For example, I wrote this book in peace and love to help you. My intention was good and noble—and in a world of massive hatred and intentional pain-inducing violence, I should feel pretty peaceful about this effort. In this sense, *the road to heaven is paved with good intentions.*

Listen to a gem of a Bible verse I discovered a few years ago. A long time ago, Israel was devastated by Babylon, an enemy country, and the temple was destroyed. King David of Israel wanted to rebuild the temple, but God did not want him to because he was a man of war. Since a temple is a place of peace, God did not want the temple built by a man who had a lot of blood on his hands! Instead, God allowed Solomon, David's son, to build the temple.

Through a prophet, the Lord said to David, "Nevertheless, you did well that it was in your heart to build a temple for me." Wow! What beauty of spirit in that moment!

As we all attempt to lead more effective lives, we endure many failures, mistakes, and rejections. To help us keep going, we must see that our hearts are in the right places. If we "do no harm," we are a cut above; if we want to build the temple, that counts as well.

We all have people we want to help who refuse our help. Despite our best efforts, people go their own way to various hells. There are temples we want to build but we cannot build them because of time, money, circumstance, lack of talent, and many varied obstacles. In my opinion, the Bible allows us to be soothed by good intentions.

Please do not distort the above Bible verse or my thoughts on good intentions, and use it as an excuse to do nothing. You will then be in the grip of fear's greatest weapon—sitting around and doing nothing—and you cannot afford that luxury.

# CHAPTER TWELVE
# MR. DISMISSIVE

◆

*(in which we battle the quicksand of despair)*

In our fight against fear, we need all the help we can get. Under this banner, I want to talk about something we all experience, although it is hard to define. Did you ever notice that you start something and you have great intentions, initial fire, and real hope that you are going to finally succeed at your goal and dreams? Did you ever notice how easily it fizzles? It's not as if you make the decision to quit—you quit before you even know it.

What I think happens here is hard to explain, but it happens. I think all of us have ponds of quicksand in our soul. That quicksand is filled with despair, cynicism, futility, and hopelessness. We have all tried to do things over and over again, and we have failed. We have failed so much that there are times when we dare not even announce to ourselves our new intentions, dreams, and goals because the quicksand is so near and so powerful.

Yet we begin again, and still so quickly, so easily, and so powerfully, we once again doubt ourselves, stumble a little, and fall into the quicksand, which sucks us in. Again, we are gone so quickly.

A better image might be that of the wind. The evil wind blows our dreams and hopes away so quickly. This is why it is so important for us to get a bit of self-control and some power going because the momentum of success gradually builds a rock of growth that can no longer be easily blown away.

The above section highlights something that occurs in our minds and hearts that is a real downer. This downer is so powerful that it makes a mockery of so much of the advice we give to one another. I will call this something a name that is simple yet powerful. Since it seems to have massive executive powers, let us call it *Mr. Dismissive*. Here's how he works:

Think of your most secret cherished vision or goal. You want to write a book, travel the world, see yourself as beautiful, or make a huge difference. Right away, the Mr. Dismissive inside of you utters his powerful, instantaneous, summary judgment, and your vision is immediately viewed as absurd, laughable, and outright foolish.

I am here to tell you that Mr. Dismissive is *so* very powerful and he can topple spiritual progress in a split second. He crushes us with speed, authority, utter confidence, and certainty.

If anyone is on our side against Mr. Dismissive, they had better be prepared for quite a fight. They will need endurance, patience, wisdom, and cunning to stand up against Mr. Dismissive. It has been said that fear stands for **F**alse **E**vidence **A**ppearing **R**eal. To anyone who knows the power of Mr. Dismissive, whose real name is FEAR, the evidence against us is absolutely true and obviously true to the whole world. Thus, fear feels like **F**ailure **E**vidence **A**bsolutely **R**eal.

To the part of us that succumbs to Mr. Dismissive, any notion that our dreams are possible seems about as likely as the most doubtful thing you can imagine. This is why therapists believe in long-term therapy. A lot of Christians believe in the devil because in the Bible, he is known as "the accuser." This part of us that succumbs to Mr. Dismissive *feels like the center of our existence. It feels like our core. It feels like this is us. If you can get where you have the awareness that this is a part of you and not the very essence and utter truth of you, you are already getting somewhere!*

Here are further things you can do that will help you battle Mr. Dismissive:

1. Trace your history and see the elements in your history that have created Mr. Dismissive in you.
2. Find friends, colleagues, therapists, relatives, and any sort of crowd so that their accumulated chorus will gradually shout down Mr. Dismissive. (Of course, one of the major tasks of any person on our Committee is to be emphatically on our side!)
3. Find the small, almost hidden, quiet voice in you that does not believe Mr. Dismissive. Remember your victories and triumphs, and play them to yourself again and again. Listen to that small, quiet voice in you that

has survived abuse, criticism, and shame. Isn't it amazing that this voice still exists and still attempts to fight even though Mr. Dismissive is so powerful?

This list looks so simple, but it is actually inviting you to a war. Step 1 sees the enemy and everything the enemy has done to you with a thousand different episodes, tools, and voices. Step 2 invites you to gather an army of troops to support you. Step 3 invites you to marshal the quiet, intense inner conviction that you don't have to lie down and listen to Mr. Dismissive anymore. This is a war.

When we are attacked by fear, it is not logical and precise. It is a sinking, all-encompassing flood that fills our soul. It's not the kind of thing you can shake off, let go of, or "just" dismiss!

When you and I go through these kinds of battles, we are fighting one of the biggest enemies of our soul. It is despair, and it is Mr. Dismissive's fastest, most efficient, and ruthless tool. In fact, Mr. Dismissive is despair incarnate.

When people are insecure or have low self-esteem, they are actually in despair. If you grow up in a troubled home and see people getting worse instead of better, despair is what saturates your being. Despair is always ready to fill your world with doubt, dismay, and perpetually rainy days.

I am writing this so you will know that *someone understands what you are up against* in your drive to be the wise, sane, peaceful, and happy Christian you want to be. It is so strengthening to be known in this way.

This is why it doesn't help to be raised by silent parents or helped by a silent therapist. *We all need massive feedback, massive support, and massive encouragement. In short, whatever help you need, you need massive amounts of it.*

Why do people need this much help?

- The world bombards us with agony, misery, doubt, and pain.
- We've received twenty-five thousand rejections by the time we are eighteen.
- We have an internal critic that never shuts up.
- The world of critics and silent supporters is bigger than the world of people who will actually tell us that we make a positive difference.

- We are scared of many sizeable enemies that add up to the "nameless face of terror" about which we all have nightmares.

The above thinking can be summed up in three words: life is hard. It is a shame that so many people miss the sanity in Christianity. Healthy Christianity has highway signs that are among the best for fighting fear, despair, and dismissive accusations from within and without.

# CHAPTER THIRTEEN
# EVERYTHING COUNTS

♦

## *(in which we battle the most subtle form of blindness)*

Want to read a whole lot of healthy theology and psychiatry in three sentences? Read this toast, worthy of the best champagne:

*Here's to everything!*
*Everything is what we need.*
*No one thing will satisfy.*

The opposite of this toast is idolatry, that old enemy of faith, where we find one inanimate thing and designate it as our god. The journey for each of us is, in part, the journey of our idolatries, where we pursue some *thing* as if it were everything. Thus, we fall in love with cars, houses, mounds of cash, and titles on our office doors. In the meantime, we neglect God, our families, and our health in pursuit of these things made of metal or paper. What's behind this pursuit is what therapists call *fusion*—the search for *the one thing* that is going to make life magical.

The healthy spiritual alternative to fusion is *everything*. The idea that everything counts is at the heart of sanity because craziness always involves a small facet of life being treated as if it is everything. Healthy spirituality does not pursue one thing, even God, at the expense of everything else—especially at the expense of our own soul or neighbor. Therefore,

*Whatever your hand finds to do, do it with all your might.*

—Ecclesiastes 9:10

You would think it would be easy to live with this kind of vitality, enthusiasm and intensity. After all, we only have one shot at life, so why not live it with all our might? But what if our hands have gotten used to the things they find to do? The familiarity of ordinary things can dull our happiness, our relationships, and our sense of well-being.

We all wake up when we hear about the sudden death of a friend or a tragic tale. The doctor tells us, "It is benign," and we live with renewed zest and wonder. Still, as the days go by, familiarity sets in and "do it with all your might" fades.

Honore de Balzac advised this about marriage—and we can apply it to every area of life:

> *Marriage should war incessantly against a monster that is the ruin of everything. This is the monster of custom.*[7]

In other words, it is easy to be married to anyone for six months. It is even easier to take anyone or anything for granted after six months.

*Anyone!*

*Anything!*

One of the clear and good intentions of spiritual habits (like worship, prayer, and preaching) is to help fight the monster of custom. Healthy spirituality is not against making our lives better or pursuing the quest for true success, but it is so, so easy to be blind to the beauty we already have.

How can we get a breath of fresh air? How can we be inspired? How can we stay awake? How can we find a passion that doesn't wreck our lives? In the next chapter, we will discuss *the fuel that helps us feel passionate and inspired. This fuel helps us feel that everything counts,* a feeling that is at the heart of healthy spirituality.

# CHAPTER FOURTEEN
# TRUE MAGIC

As we walk before God in the light of life, we will find wisdom, peace, and sacred meaning, all of which move us toward love. The more we walk in healthy spirituality, the more we are walking closer to our ideals.

Deep inside, we all carry around our "ego ideal," which is how we want to be, the vision of what we are trying to live up to. We have to live up to our ego ideal, or we become irritated and overwhelmed. Depression is often a measure of the gap between how we want life to be and what life is actually like. Therefore, we have to do more than take a pill to get out of mental anguish. We must change our life.

As we change, we head toward a harmony, a quiet peace, a deep confidence, and a calm reverence. We also head toward a reality that is the secret within healthy spirituality and the true magic that fuels a happy life.

It is one unsurpassable quality that is both the result of and the fuel for passionate living. It is:

**ENERGY!**

Energy is the most underrated and supremely beautiful result of living a good life. Why should you cut down on drinking, over-eating, feeling guilty, overworking, embracing hatred, and doing the other things that bog you down? Why should you add water, exercise, peace, limits, and love to your life? Because you will gain *energy*.

Energy is the most undervalued commodity of our day. It is one of the qualities that we should look for in a therapist or minister. We all admire people who are confident, decisive, and wise. We all admire leaders. Energy is an underlying attribute that we often fail to notice in those we admire. We could call it by other names—vitality, power, charisma—but it is the quiet, steady fuel that we need.

Any sane life endorses and feeds off of energy. Likewise, any healthy spirituality, including Christianity, offers a breath of fresh air, renewal, and revival. Exhaustion is a greater enemy to spiritual health than we can imagine. Fighting fatigue involves looking after our bodies, which are, in Christian terms, "the temple of the Holy Spirit."

Here are ten guidelines that will help you acquire more spiritual energy. If you *work at this,* you will gain freshness and vitality. Energy will beget more energy, and you will know the beauty of what I am talking about.

1. Get plenty of sleep. Sleep is the number one factor in mental health.
2. Exercise is *by far* the best drug. How much exercise are you getting?
3. Go for a walk. Walking is an example of all the free things we can do that are so wonderful for us.
4. Visit a nursing home or intensive care unit. Then you'll see what a great day you are already having.
5. Listen to Mozart.
6. Drink plenty of pure water and eat healthy food.
7. Hang around lively people of all sorts.
8. Vary your routines.
9. Pay careful attention to yourself whenever you cry.
10. Pray—for energy.

As Isaiah said,

*Those who wait upon the Lord shall renew their strength. They shall mount up with wings like eagles, they shall run and not be weary, they shall walk and not to be faint.*

—Isaiah 40:31

We also must connect to the world inside us and the world outside us if we are to gain energy. Here are ten more guidelines for accomplishing this goal:

1. Examine and manage the "oil well" inside you. The oil well is the image I use for the accumulated damages that lurk within your soul. For example, maybe you are bitter because of the hard knocks life has handed

you. You can see how your past has shaped you in this regard. It is energizing to understand this, to feel sorry for yourself, and then to live in a way that makes you less bitter.

2. Allow yourself to get angry sometimes. Anger has within it the seeds of self-respect. You get angry because you don't like being hurt.

3. Watch out for pointless complaining and habitual whining. This could lead to self-pity, which is a long, slow poison! (Do you swallow this poison? Ask the Committee if self-pity is your best friend.)

4. Let your sexuality flow out of a natural passion as opposed to giving into the compulsive habit that lives as if sex is everything.

5. Limit your alcohol consumption. Alcohol is a depressant. It actually disconnects you from yourself and from others—although it feels quite the opposite. How much are you drinking?

6. Consider the possibility that you are doing better than you think.

7. Give yourself enough time to think and ponder. It is very refreshing to do so. Most of us don't value our brains enough.

8. Correct your money problems, as they are a real drain. Correcting them will give you energy.

9. Living well is the best revenge. Help yourself to triumph over your past and all that has hurt you.

10. Put into effect something about yourself that you must stop doing in order to have energy. After all, you know something about yourself that only you can know.

This is all doable, but it is hard to break the habits, thoughts, and feelings that have sapped us of our energy. We need the help of honest, affirming people who will tell us our faults, and, *more importantly, tell us our strengths.*

Here's a story in that regard: About ten years ago, I was golfing with a friend named Ralston, who is a superb golfer. It was our first time playing together, and on the eleventh fairway, we had the following conversation:

Ralston: Bob, did anybody ever teach you how to play golf?

Bob: No, not really.

| | |
|---|---|
| Ralston: | Would you like to learn? |
| Bob: | Sure. |
| Ralston: | Well, let me tell you why I'd be willing to teach you. First off, on the first nine, I gave you a couple of suggestions. You listened to me and put them into practice. Secondly, you have tremendous hand-eye coordination, and there's no reason you shouldn't be playing in the low eighties. |
| Bob: | (stunned) Really? |
| Ralston: | Yes, so let's get to work. Let's look at your clubs. I suspect they are trash (they were). You need to know that you overuse your pitching wedge and you don't really go for the flag. You hold back! |

Ralston got through to me because he offered me accurate challenges *and amazing support.* Consequently, I dropped ten strokes or more off my game that summer. Now it is difficult to say what actually led to my improved golf game. Was it getting rid of my reliance on my pitching wedge? Was it playing more golf? I'm tempted to say it was the belief he had instilled in me as a golfer with his affirmation of my coordination!

Who knows? What all the research shows, though, is that growth happens when we are challenged to be our best, given tools to do our best (including the belief we can do it), and then go and do it. This is crucial because life is not a breeze and we must be prepared for how difficult it can be. Spiritual energy is the master tool we need to face life's difficulties and the fuel we need to appreciate its beauties.

One of the tricks in acquiring healthy spirituality is staying open to the surprises that will come your way. That day on the golf course, was I expecting to receive such fine challenge and support? Not really! I was hoping for a hole in one. Instead, spiritual truth snuck up on me, as it often does to us all.

Grace is unexpected good surprises. Sanity is noticing them. Healthy spirituality feeds off the good surprises.

Even on a golf course, wonderful surprises come along to challenge us and support us as we prepare to do our best, love our neighbor, and even prepare to meet our God.

# CONCLUSION

◆

*(in which I invite you to join my Committee)*

It is my deepest hope that the highways signs built in this book have made you more aware of the universal wisdom in Christian faith. In a crazy world, we need all the wisdom we can get. I think it is really possible to be a Christian and still be sane—because many of the "dangers" of our current Christian mindset can be challenged by highway signs we have found in the Bible.

As most of us know, being a Christian is about love. Sanity is about love, too. When we are sane, we see what matters and we are able to put things in a loving perspective. When we are sane, we love others and ourselves with a bigger awareness that comes out of love. When we are crazy, our world gets small, and we become consumed by our anger, jealousy, lust, greed, disgust, or hatred. Then we consume others in our smallness.[8]

Spirituality is about the bigger picture. Spirituality is ultimately about love. In this respect, healthy spirituality matches the soul of psychotherapy because "psychotherapy is in essence a cure through love" (Freud). At the heart of the Christian faith is an invitation to love—to love God, our neighbor, nature, and ourselves. This invitation pulls us to a bigger world and invites us away from a "no-longer-useful-littleness."

I hope that this book, especially its highway signs, has alerted you to dangers you may not have previously taken into account. More importantly, I hope you see more of the beauty and profound wisdom that is part of the Christian heritage. If that is the case, I have done you a favor.

In return, would you please do me a favor? Please contact me at my website: (FindWisdomNow.com) if you have questions, ideas, suggestions, criticisms, and compliments in relation to this book. **I'd love to hear from you!** Help make my world bigger, **join my Committee**, and help me be more Christian—which is to be more sane!

# APPENDIX A

# YOU CAN'T JUST "LET IT GO": WHAT I'VE LEARNED FROM TEN YEARS OF BEING A PSYCHOTHERAPIST

A husband dies and a widow is left in her grief. A mother is psychotic and fills her child with the undeniable fact that the child's sole purpose in life is to live for the mother. For the thousandth time, a teenage boy asks his parents for something fair and is curtly told no, and for the thousandth time, he walks away invisible and defeated. A weary fifty-three-year-old woman has no money, no skills, and a husband she hates who has money and skills. A thirteen-year-old looks in the mirror and sees the ugliness of her body weight that the kids have been taunting her about for the past six years.

I think of these people and others like them, and although I'm not a gambling man, I would bet you one thing: within one year, each of these people has heard someone say, "Just let it go! Just let it go!" Before this paper is over, I hope to convince you that to say, "Just let it go" is another mark of our daily, ordinary insanity. In fact, almost every time I hear someone say, "Just let it go," I think of it as a minor tragedy.

Now I could come at this simply from a language perspective. Notice how you can put the word "just" before any amazing, difficult thing:

- Just get on a tightrope and walk over Niagara Falls.
- Just go in and demand a raise from your boss.
- Just tell your wife you cheated on her.

I could just simply say that "just" should be removed from our vocabulary. Instead, I want to come at this from what I've learned from ten years of being a psychotherapist.

I believe I have learned a great deal from the immense, holy privilege of sitting with people as they describe their inner world of pain, secrets, joys, agonies, ideals, disappointments, and hopes. I have learned far more, of course, than I can say, but today, I want to say just one thing: you can't just let it go. Here is why.

If you sit for a while with the widow in her grief, the trapped wife, the young man who was always refused, the woman who lives for her mother, and the teenager who knows beyond a shadow of a doubt that she is ugly, you will eventually (if you do not condemn them) get to hear that they have an inner world, whose broken reality is as powerful as the brokenness of diabetes, a torn hamstring, or a fractured femur. If you sit for a while with these people, you will discover that their inner landscape is filled with realities as powerful as the realities of the earth, sea, and sky.

The widow, in her grief, is filled with an emptiness the size of the Grand Canyon. The young man never heard is as unseen as the fish at the bottom of the sea—and he expects a "no" just as much as the fish expects darkness. The unhappily married woman is in a trap that feels as imprisoning as Green Haven to an inmate, and even though the walls don't look as gray and thick in her bungalow, the walls in her mind are as imposing as the walls in Stormville. The teenage girl is as dazed by the spell of the teasing of others as is a driver making his way through the London fog. The woman taught to live only for her mother does it with the certainty and obedience with which salmon swim upstream.

A concise way to put all this is to say that people have character, and the Latin word for character comes from the word "rock." You can't just let go of a rock. It takes time, skill, effort, and dynamite to move rock. Our grief, fear, tragic obedience, and crazy viewpoints are rocks, flowers, mud, grass, and lakes that fill us internally—and to move them too quickly risks a landslide. If there is a landslide, we risk the emptiness of psychosis.

It is my conviction that we therapists, ministers, and help workers of various sorts—particularly those who write self-help books—often forget the daze of the London fog inside the highways of our souls. This oversight has more consequences than I can name, but I will name some of them.

The most serious consequence of our mistaken viewpoint is that we do not accurately assess what people are up against, and, thus, we lead the already well-blamed victims to feel even weaker, more stupid, and more inhuman. For example, take the notion of secondary gain. It is a basic, wise therapeutic viewpoint that teaches therapists to look for the benefit in the pathology or (to use therapeutic terms) the pleasure of the sin. In my opinion, we have so emphasized this point that the victims will often say long before the therapist does, "Well, I guess I must want to live this way."

In light of our emphasis on people *wanting* their illnesses, I think we should invite William Safire or the composers of the *Oxford English Dictionary* to come up with two definitions of "want." Want #1 would be the clear, precise wants we all have, as in "I want a piece of watermelon. I do not want lima beans." Want #2 should be reserved for the murky, unfair, unjust, confused, ambivalent wants, as in "I want to stay with my jerk of a husband inside these prison walls because I am absolutely convinced that I will be a bag lady on the street if I walk out these doors." In the latter, the choice is between overcooked lima beans and undercooked lima beans—and should we really be using the word "want," as in watermelon want, in this case?

If we do not change our language to reflect a wiser understanding, we will continue to describe person's unconscious world as if it has a clarity and intentionality that does not reflect how the person feels. As a result, we as ministers and therapists will not come close to conveying the seductive and confusing spell of illusions, addictions, and cherished ambitions. In my opinion, this is why most discussion of President Clinton's behavior was so shrill and self-righteous—we refuse to see what the Bible openly acknowledges as the "deceitfulness of sin." We forget Homer's warning about the power of the Sirens' song to pull our ship into the rocks.

A second consequence of our underestimation of the power of character, habit, and early training is that current therapists are often very scared of dependent clients. Now I know that managed care will not pay for two visits per week unless they see a truckload of paperwork, but in my opinion, it follows that once we see the power of the fog and the rock, we will automatically and naturally welcome the idea that clients automatically and naturally need more time and assistance from therapists who offer dynamite, sunshine, and a whole new world.

New worlds do not come easy and fast. The wise minister, Rabbi, or therapist knows we all need all the help we can get. In that sense, I have noticed in many of my colleagues and in myself the growing realization that "it takes a village to raise a child." Community is what adults need as well. One therapy hour per week, one worship service per week is not enough. Actually, we are all very dependent!

A third consequence to our "just let it go" mentality is that we will not notice the tremendous importance of various tools that are absolutely essential when we can't just let it go. The wise healer knows that time, more time, and even more time is needed. Also, patience will be absolutely essential, especially the kind in the Bible that comes from the Greek word *macrothumos*. *Macro* means "long" and *thumos* means "passion," so to be patient is to have a long passion.

Another necessary tool is what I call "parallel sympathy," the ability to recognize that if we can't lose ten pounds, stop biting our nails, or be on time for breakfast, then it isn't so easy to just say no to heroin! I assume, without actual experience, that heroin is more of a high than biting one's nails, and cocaine is more addictive than lima beans.

In this connection, let me say a word about forgiveness and parallel empathy. Have you ever noticed how easy it is for you and me to ask Joe to forgive the guy who punched him while we haven't forgiven a less harmful sin? Have you ever noticed in the Bible how St. Paul, St. Peter, or St. James invites us to forgive and "honor all men" and "do not return reviling for reviling," and then in the next chapter they are calling their enemies "wild beasts that are born to be caught and killed"?

A final treasured tool that becomes more indispensable if we can't just let go of our fears, guilt, and rock-solid inner world is the unacknowledged helper of humanity. Here I speak of action—the ability of the soul, body, and mind to move toward actions that create a new world over time. The widow gets out and connects with people. The unseen young man takes a risk by asking for a date. The young woman finds new and better people to live for than her psychotic mother. The teenager finds out by talking to others that a boy finds her pretty. The woman inside her marital prison starts hiding money under her mattress and at least gets to go on a trip to visit her brother, who will tell her a hundred times that she deserves better.

People need insight into their unconscious, and they need healers to journey with them. However, action repeated again and again is the indispensable creator of better worlds—inside us and outside us. If life is as easy as "just let it go" dictates, we will underestimate the importance of repeated action. Thus, we will go to Barnes & Noble looking for the books that promise us the easy path and easy secrets to the new world so we won't have to notice how cruel the world is and how powerful evil is. We will then underestimate the beauty and wisdom of the Judeo-Christian tradition and the psychotherapeutic tradition—for both traditions have for centuries insisted on the fight that is spirituality and thereby have unceasingly emphasized habits, practices, daily rituals, and prayer.

"The way is hard that leads to life," said Jesus, in the Sermon on the Mount. In other words, you can't "just let it go." Our victories are hard-won. The fog is thick and moves off the coast slowly.

It will be interesting to hear from my readers and listeners what they think of this rock and fog of a paper. I am easily willing to be kinder to lima beans. The ironic thing, of course, is that much of what I have thought here, I really treasure—and I just can't let it go. Still, I welcome your light, wisdom, and dynamite in response.

*—From a lecture delivered on the occasion of the merger of Northeast Counseling Center and FRMH of Duchess and Orange, and the author's installation as Associate Director of the newly merged and named Northeast Counseling Center, June 5, 2001.*

# APPENDIX B
# FIFTY-TWO ADDITIONAL HIGHWAY SIGNS

Here are fifty-two more Bible verses that would look great on the highway signs of life. They are timeless, totally useful, easy to understand, and applicable to every person in the world. In fact, here's some quick spiritual advice for these busy days: Take these Bible verses—one by one—and reflect on each of them for a week at a time. It will add true magic to your life.

*So whatever you wish that men would do to you, do so to them; for this is the law and the prophets.*

—Matthew 7:12

*Wisdom is justified by all her children.*

—Matthew 11:19

*Leave simpleness and live, and walk in the way of insight.*

—Proverbs 9:6

*Let your speech always be gracious, seasoned with salt, so that you may know how you ought to answer every one.*

—Colossians 4:6

*If any one thinks he is religious, and does not bridle his tongue but deceives his heart, this man's religion is vain. Religion that is pure and undefiled before God is this: to visit orphans and widows in their affliction, and to keep oneself unstained from the world.*

—James 1:27

*Let love be genuine; hate what is evil; hold fast to what is good; love one another with brotherly affection; outdo one another in showing honor.*

—Romans 12:9, 10

*How precious is thy steadfast love. O God!*
*The children of men take refuge in the shadow of thy wings.*
*They feast on the abundance of thy house*
*And thou givest them drink from the water of thy delights.*
*For with thee is the fountain of life;*
*In thy light do we see light.*

—Psalms 36:7–9

*Love does not insist on its own way; it is not irritable or resentful; it does not rejoice at wrong, but rejoices in the right.*

—1 Corinthians 13: 5, 6

*Be angry, but do not sin; do not let the sun go down on your anger.*

—Ephesians 4:26

*But the fruit of the Spirit is love, joy, peace, patience, kindness, goodness, faithfulness, gentleness, self-control; against such there is no law.*

—Galatians 5:22, 23

*Test everything.*

—1 Thessalonians 5:21

*Do not occupy yourselves with myths and endless genealogies which promote speculations ... the aim of our charge is love that issues from a pure heart and a good conscience and sincere faith. Certain persons by swerving from these have wandered away into vain discussion, without understanding either what they are saying or the things about which they make assertions.*

—1 Timothy 4:7

*Let every person be quick to hear, slow to speak, slow to anger.*

—James 1:19

*Now we know in part; in heaven we shall understand fully, even as we have been fully understood. So faith, hope, love abide, these three; but the greatest of these is love.*

—1 Corinthians 13:12, 13

*Rejoice with those who rejoice, weep with those who weep.*

—Romans 12:15

*All of you, have unity of spirit, sympathy, love of the brethren, a tender heart, and a humble mind. Do not return evil for evil or reviling for reviling; but on the contrary bless, for to this you have been called, that you may obtain a blessing. He that would love life and see good days, let him keep his tongue from evil and his lips from speaking guile. Let him turn away from evil and do right; let him seek peace and pursue it.*

—1 Peter 3:8–11

*He who does not love does not know God, for God is love.*

—1 John 4:8

*In the beginning, God created the heavens and the earth ... And God created man and woman in his own image ... And God saw everything that he made, and behold, it was very good.*

—Genesis 1:1, 27, 31

*You shall not follow a multitude to do evil.*

—Exodus 23:2

*Every good endowment and every perfect gift is from above, coming down from the Father of lights with whom there is no variation or shadow due to change.*

—James 1:15

*Therefore, do not be anxious about tomorrow, for tomorrow will be anxious for itself. Let the day's own trouble be sufficient for the day.*

—Matthew 6:34

*You shall honor the face of an old man.*

—Leviticus 19:32

*And let us not grow weary in well-doing, for in due season we shall reap, if we do not lose heart. So then, as we have opportunity let us do good to all people, and especially to those who are of the household of faith.*

—Galatians 6:9, 10

*Repay no one evil for evil, but take thought for what is noble in the sight of all. If possible, so far as it depends on you, live peaceably with all.*

—Romans 12:17, 8

*For everything created by God is good, and nothing is to be rejected if it is received with thanksgiving; for then it is consecrated by the word of God and prayer.*

—1 Timothy 4:4, 5

*Teach us, O Lord, to number our days that we might find a heart of wisdom.*

—Psalms 90:12

*Look carefully then how you walk, not as unwise people but as wise, making the most of the time, because the days are evil.*

—Ephesians 5:15

*Who is wise and understanding among you? By his good life let him show his works in the meekness of wisdom.*

—James 3:13

*You shall not oppress a hired servant who is poor and needy, whether he is one of your brethren or a sojourner; you shall give him his hire on the day he earns it, before the sun goes down (for he is poor and sets his heart upon it); lest he cry against you to the Lord, and it be sin in you.*

—Deuteronomy 25:14, 15

*By rejecting conscience, certain persons have made shipwreck of their faith.*
—1 Timothy 1:18

*Jesus wept.*
—John 11:35

*Stand by the roads, and look,*
*And ask for the ancient paths,*
*where the good way is; and walk in it,*
*and find rest for your souls.*
—Jeremiah 6:16

*Above all, hold unfailing your love for one another, since love covers a multitude of sins.*
—1 Peter 4:8

*If you meet your enemy's ox going astray, you shall bring it back to him. If you see the ox of one who hates you lying under its burden, you shall refrain from leaving him with it, you shall help him to lift it up.*
—Exodus 23:4

*O Lord, my heart is not lifted up,*
*My eyes are not raised too high;*
*I do not occupy myself with things*
*Too great and too marvelous for me.*
*But I have calmed and quieted my soul,*
*Like a child quieted at its mother's breast.*
—Psalms 131:1, 2

*For you can all prophesy one by one, so that all may learn and all may be encouraged; and the spirits of prophets are subject to prophets. For God is not a God of confusion but of peace.*
—I Corinthians 14:31, 32

*Thou hast made men and women a little less than God, and dost crown them with glory and honor.*

—Psalms 8:5

*We aim for what is honorable, not only in the Lord's sight, but also in the sight of men and women.*

—2 Corinthians 8:21

*He who gets wisdom loves his own soul;*
*He who keeps understanding will prosper.*

—Proverbs 19:3

*If any of you lacks wisdom, let him ask God, who gives to all men generously and without reproaching, and it will be given him.*

—James 1:5

*And the Lord's servant must not be quarrelsome but kindly to every one, an apt teacher, forbearing, correcting his opponents with gentleness.*

—1 Timothy 24, 25

*Let no one boast of their varied groups and forget others. For all things are yours. (Author's paraphrase)*

—I Corinthians 3:21

*As you do not know how the spirit comes to the bones in the womb of a woman with child, so you do not know the work of God who makes everything.*

—Ecclesiastes 11:5

*God has not given us a spirit of fear, but of power, love, and self-control.*

—2 Timothy 1:7

*When a stranger sojourns with you in your land, you shall not do him wrong. The stranger who sojourns with you shall be to you as the native among you, and you shall love him as yourself; for you were strangers in the land of Egypt. I am the Lord your God.*

—Leviticus 18:33, 34

*Let your yes be yes and your no be no, anything more than this comes from evil.*

—Matthew 5:37

*You shall open wide your hand to the needy and to the poor.*

—Deuteronomy 15:11

*Do not withhold good from those to whom it is due,*
*When it is in your power to do it.*
*Do not say to your neighbor—"go and come again,*
*Tomorrow I will give it"—when you have it with you.*

—Proverbs 3:27, 28

*The earth is the Lord's and the fullness thereof, the world and those who dwell therein.*

—Psalms 24:1

*Jesus said, A new commandment I give to you, that you love one another ... By this shall all people know you are my disciples, if you have love for one another.*

—John 13:34, 35

*And the city of heaven has no need of sun or moon to shine upon it, for the glory of God is its light. By its light shall the nations walk; and the kings of the earth shall bring their glory into it, and its gates shall never be shut by day—and there shall be no night there; they shall bring into it the glory and honor of the nations.*

—Revelation 21:23–26

*Then I saw a new heaven and a new earth; for the first heaven and the first earth had passed away, and the sea was no more. And I saw the holy city, new Jerusalem, coming down out of heaven from God, prepared a bride adorned for her husband; and I heard a loud voice from the throne saying, "Behold, the dwelling of God is with men and women. He will dwell with them and they shall be his people, and God himself will be with them; he will wipe away every tear from their eyes, and death shall be no more, neither shall there be mourning nor crying nor pain anymore, for the former things have passed away." And he who sat upon the throne said, "Behold, I make all things new."*

—Revelation 21:1–5

# APPENDIX C
# ADDITIONAL HIGHWAY SIGNS FROM PROVERBS

In my opinion, *Proverbs* is one of the wisest books ever written. Here are some gems for you:

*By wisdom a house is built,*
*and by understanding it is established;*
*By knowledge the rooms are filled,*
*with all precious and pleasant riches. (24:3, 4)*

*I, wisdom, dwell in prudence,*
*and I find knowledge and discretion. (8:12)*

*Keep your heart with all vigilance,*
*for from it flow the springs of life. (4:23)*

*If you are in debt, save yourself like a gazelle from the hunter,*
*like a bird from the hand of the fowler. (6:1, 5 my translation)*

*Wise men lay up knowledge,*
*but the babbling of a fool brings ruin near. (10:14)*

*When words are many, transgression is not lacking,*
*but he who restrains his lips is prudent. (10:19)*

*Where there is no guidance, a people falls;*
*but in an abundance of counselors there is safety. (11:14)*

*Anxiety in a man's heart weighs him down,*
*but a good word makes him glad.* (12:25)

*There is one whose rash words are like sword thrusts,*
*but the tongue of the wise brings healing.* (12:18)

*The soul of the sluggard craves, and gets nothing,*
*while the soul of the diligent is richly supplied.* (13:4)

*Wealth hastily gotten will dwindle,*
*but he who gathers little by little will increase it.* (13:11)

*Hope deferred makes the heart sick,*
*but a desire fulfilled is a tree of life.* (13:11)

*The simple believes everything,*
*but the prudent looks where he is going.* (14:15)

*A man of quick temper acts foolishly,*
*but a man of discretion is patient.* (14:17)

*In all toil there is profit,*
*but mere talk tends only to want.* (14:23)

*He who oppresses a poor man insults his Maker,*
*but he who is kind to the poor honors him.* (14:31)

*A soft answer turns away wrath,*
*but a harsh word stirs up anger.* (15:1)

*A gentle tongue is a tree of life.* (15:4)

*A cheerful heart has a continual feast.* (15:15)

*Better is a dinner of herbs where love is*
*than a fatted ox and hatred with it.* (15:17)

*To make an apt answer is a joy to a man,*
*and a word in season, how good it is!* (15:23)

*He who ignores instruction despises himself.* (15:32)

*To get wisdom is better than gold* (16:16)

*He who is slow to anger is better than the mighty,
and he who conquers himself is mightier
than he who conquers a city.* (16:32)

*The beginning of strife is like letting out water;
so quit before the quarrel breaks out.* (17:14)

*A man of understanding sets his face towards wisdom,
but the eyes of a fool are on the ends of the earth.* (17:24)

*A fool takes no pleasure in understanding,
but only in expressing his opinion.* (18:2)

*He who is slack in his work is a brother to him who destroys.* (18:9)

*It is not good for a man to be without knowledge,
and he who makes haste with his feet misses his way.* (19:2)

*He who is kind to the poor lends to the Lord,
and he will repay him for his deed.* (19:17)

*Wine is a mocker, strong drink a brawler;
and whoever is led astray by it is not wise.* (20:1)

*It is an honor for a man to keep aloof from strife;
but every fool will be quarreling.* (20:3)

*A word fitly spoken is like apples of gold in a setting of silver.* (25:11)

*A man who bears false witness against his neighbor,
is like a war club, or a sword, or a sharp arrow.* (25:18)

*Better is open rebuke than hidden love.* (27:5)

*Iron sharpens iron, and one person sharpens another.* (27:17)

# APPENDIX D
# A LOVE LETTER

I recently resigned as pastor of Netherwood Baptist Church in Salt Point, New York after fifteen years of pastoral ministry. I include a copy of my final handout to the congregation to further illustrate the major tenets of this book.

---

October 1, 2006

It has been fifteen years since I started preaching at Netherwood Baptist Church. In that time, we have had countless sacred moments of laughter, tears, learning, and love. All in all, our time together has been filled with plenty of glory. This final handout is a note of gratitude to you and an attempt to sum up the top fifteen things I have said (and tried to live) in my fifteen years of ministry. Most of all, this is a love letter.

To best convey this, I will go through our order of service with you.

1) Our worship begins with a call to worship. It is an invitation. It is not an order, a command, or an act of force. People are freely invited to come and worship God. In my ministry with you, I have endeavored to create a community of freedom where we do what we want out of our unique gifts, passion, and insights. Christians believe in "the priesthood of all believers," in which the community of faith is shaped by the wisdom and voice of all the people.

Thankfully, we have avoided the forceful, dictatorial, and scared atmosphere that exists in so many churches. Our church has not been run by a know-it-all attitude or any slave-making force. As we all know, anyway, the more people try to run our lives, the more we rebel.

So, may you continue to respect the freedom of people and invite them, in freedom, to worship God and follow His ways.

*Where the Spirit of the Lord is, there is freedom.*

*—2 Corinthians 3:17*

2) As people come to worship, they stand before the door to a church. It is their choice whether or not to open that door. We are all deeply shaped by the doors we open and the doors we leave closed. When we open a door to something and walk in its space, we learn about that something. Thus, Bill "Laz" Gleason knows gardens and Paul Johnson knows bridges. Likewise, when people open the door to pursue God, they learn and grow in that direction. Just as it takes time and willingness to learn gardens and bridges, it takes time and willingness to know God—and there are many people who speak about things (especially in the area of religion) who have not spent any time finding out about that thing of which they speak. Don't forget that!

3) After we walk through the door and hear the Call to Worship, we sing a hymn. Hymns are about gratitude and counting our blessings. Hymns are about our efforts to "praise God from whom all blessings flow." Hymns often speak about life's troubles, so this gratitude is not blind to the darkness within our existence. We sing hymns because we need to practice gratitude. Is there anything better for you than gratitude?

I am grateful to God for you—and I am grateful for all the love and respect you have shown me.

4) The "Prayer of Invocation" follows the hymn, at which time we invite God to touch our lives in this service. Since God is the giver of all good gifts, we should not fear His touch because it uplifts, refreshes, and inspires. God is love—so we invoke His work of love in our lives. Alas, the story of all of us is the story of us forgetting God and chasing after (invoking) other things that we think are better for us.

5) With thanks, we next say the Lord's Prayer, so we can get our bearings in these beautiful words. "Our Father" is good for us because He is good to us. "Hallowed be His name" because He is the author of all good gifts. So may "Thy kingdom come and Thy will be done, on earth as it is in heaven" because it's not

being done on earth, and we are making a mess. Yes, "give us this day our daily bread," and may we take it one day at a time and help our neighbors get bread, too.

So "forgive us our sins as we forgive others" and "lead us not into temptation" because we've already blown it enough this week. In fact, "deliver us from evil" because there *is* evil—and it is so big and harmful that we need "Your kingdom" and "Your power" and "Your glory" to save us!

The Lord's Prayer is one of the glorious gems of the Christian life. Being a Christian is about finding gems—especially the gem of Jesus, especially the gem of people.

6) We next sing "The Gloria Patri." This ancient hymn is a reminder that Christians have been singing to the Father, the Son, and the Holy Spirit for more than two thousand years. Our faith has not been "here today and gone tomorrow." It was handed to us by people who died to spread its message. It was handed to us by good people "of whom the world is not worthy" (Hebrews 11). Be thankful "for all the saints," a multitude that no man can number, who have been singing this hymn for centuries. The church is not three people or just the Netherwood Baptist Church in Salt Point. It is a "great cloud of witnesses" that can strengthen us.

7) The Children's time allows us to see why Jesus blessed the children and said, "Of such is the Kingdom of Heaven." Why are children the essence of Heaven? I think Jesus loved their ability to live in the present and to imagine and have faith. He knew their innocence and beauty reflects the fact that we are made in "the image of God." Who can look at a child and not have more faith, wonder, and gratitude?

8) After this comes the announcements and prayer requests, where we are reminded that we are a community of faith with upcoming events, birthdays, celebrations, dreams, and goals. So ... come to the Sunday School Picnic, notice that a Trustee meeting has been scheduled, volunteer to be a deacon, or go visit Myrtle in the nursing home—not because we want to work you to death ... not because you haven't done significant stuff at work and at home this week ... but because this church stands for the ideals and values that make life worth living—and we need your help and effort to make this community a gem.

In my fifteen years here, the church has grown in terms of people. The building is in top shape. The grounds look marvelous. Many of our prayer requests have been backed up by the actions of the Diaconate, the Thimble Club, individuals, and the Sunday School—as we have sent food, Christmas shoe boxes, and cards to hurting people. We've done better than Enron financially as the trustees have managed the finances so honorably and well. Here's a toast to the memory of Bob Mausler, who insisted—as only he could—that we do more in terms of investments and reserves. Thanks to all!

9) We then pray because Jesus has taught us to pray. Prayer is way better than so many of the things we do, think, and feel. Stop those things before you ever stop praying! We pray because it is us wishing our best and God's best for people who aren't having the best time of it. As most of us have experienced, when we are lying in a hospital bed, it is so comforting to know that people are praying for us.

10) We then take the offering because everything matters in this life, including money—and money is a powerful tool of love! The invitation to give is in the spirit of Jesus, who said, "God loves a cheerful giver" and "Freely you have received, freely give." We then sing the Doxology with its "Praise God from whom all blessings flow." Who cannot give freely and cheerfully, given all the blessings that have been given to us?

One of the gifts that I have given you is the word "all" because I believe God is the giver of "all" good things, and our faith should make us bigger people with huge hearts of compassion and huge brains filled with wisdom. "In Christ are hid all the treasures of wisdom and knowledge." (Colossians 2:3) "The earth is the Lord's and the fullness thereof." (Psalms 46:1)

There is nothing more contradictory than a petty Christian! God save us from petty churches!

11) After the offering, we say a prayer of thanksgiving—and one of the things we are thankful for is one another. Hence, we have often had a wild five minutes when we greet one another with hugs, holy kisses, and handshakes because "They'll know we are Christians by our love." Period. End of story.

12) Next is the Bible reading. I have always highlighted the verses that are universal, easy to understand, and apply to our daily lives. I'm sorry that I have not been able to grasp most of the Book of Revelation or the dreams of Daniel—but I'm not sorry I've showed you Proverbs, Philippians 4, Jesus' call to "Come and have breakfast" (a few days after he died), the Log verse, "Do unto others as you would have them do unto you," and countless other gems.

13) I am so honored that you have found my sermons (which follow after the Bible reading) to be interesting, helpful, and inspiring. Do forgive the jokes that didn't really fit in. At least we laughed together. Forgive the times when I was too tired because I had driven all over Creation or stayed up to watch *24*.

Do not rest until you find a new preacher who can preach with power and enthusiasm—because preaching is at the heart of Christian worship, because preaching is about the value of the human soul, the glories of Easter, the hope of eternal life, and the transforming power of love. Thank you for the privilege of allowing me to preach about such sacred and life-giving realities.

14) We then have a final hymn, which is in response to the sermon. We close our worship, as we began it, with gratitude.

15) We end with the *Benediction*, which comes from the Latin word for *blessing*. Our mission as Christians is to bless. I have easily blessed you all every week, and will continue to do so in my heart forever, because you have been so, so good to me (and kind, respectful, gracious, forgiving, and affirming) that as I type these words now, I am actually crying like a baby, with tears running down my face, as my soul knows that I love you and you have loved me—and that is what it is all about.

With all my respect, gratitude, and love in Christ,<br>
Bob Beverley

# ENDNOTES

1. Phillips, *The Seven Laws of Money*, p.27
2. Winget, *Shut Up, Stop Whining & Get a Life*, 101.
3. Maya Angelou in a personal interview on *The Oprah Winfrey Show*, April 2005 as cited on the Web site, Pure-Essence.net
4. There is a whole book of theology in this rowing parable. John Ashcroft refers to it as originating from "some missionary." See an interview with him called "A Patriot of Faith" on the Web site for *Regent University Christian Leader Magazine*.
5. Lewis, *The Problem of Pain*, p.115
6. Remnick, p.144ff
7. Winget, p.139.
8. I am indebted to Ron Peck, Sr. of Pawling, New York, for first introducing me to the whole concept of smallness when it comes to human perception and behavior.

# A BIBLIOGRAPHY OF SORTS

This book is my attempt to show how much the Bible has influenced my life. In particular, I would "push" and endorse that you read Proverbs, the Psalms, Ecclesiastes, Micah 6, the Gospel of Luke, 1 Corinthians 13, Romans 12, Philippians 4, and the book of James—if you want to receive massive doses of wisdom and sanity. These books are good places to begin if you are new to the Bible. The book of Proverbs, especially, cannot be praised highly enough for its down-to-earth wisdom.

I have also read virtually everything written by the following authors, and I am grateful for the ways in which their wisdom has shaped my life. In a way, they are my Committee. So, thanks to C. S. Lewis, Frederick Buechner, Robert Farrar Capon, Walker Percy, Thomas Howard, Iris Murdoch, Balthasar Gracian, Barbara Brown Taylor, David Allen, Phillips Brooks, and David Schnarch.

The following specific sources have been noteworthy in my spiritual journey:

Abraham, Jay. 2000. *Getting Everything You Can Out of All You've Got*. New York: St. Martins Press.

Allen, David. 2001. *Getting Things Done*. New York: Penguin Books.

Barth, Karl. 1957. *Church Dogmatics* Vol. 3, Pt. 4. Edinburgh: T&T Clark.

Brooks, Phillips. 1899. *Lectures on Preaching*. New York: Dutton.

Buechner, Frederick. 1977. *Telling the Truth*. San Francisco: Harper & Row.

———. 1982. *The Sacred Journey*. San Francisco: Harper & Row.

———. 1983. *Now and Then*. San Francisco: Harper & Row.

———. 1984. *The Book of Bebb*. New York: Atheneum.

———. 1991. *Telling Secrets*. New York: Harper Collins.

———. 1999. *Eyes of the Heart*. New York: Harper Collins.

Capon, Robert Farrar. 1965. *Bed and Board*. New York: Simon & Schuster.

———. 1967. *Supper of the Lamb*. New York: Doubleday.

Gibran, Kahil. 1994. *The Prophet*. New York: Alfred A. Knopf.

Gracian, Balthasar. 1993. *The Art of Worldly Wisdom*. New York: Shambhala.

Grudin, Robert. 1982. *Time and the Art of Living*. New York: Harper & Row.

Hills, L. Rust. 1972. *How to Do Things Right*. Boston: David R. Godine.

Hogan, Kevin, and James Speakman. 2006. *Covert Persuasion*. Hoboken, NJ: John Wiley & Sons.

Hollon, Frank Turner. 2002. *The God File*. San Francisco: MacAdam/Cage Publishing.

Howard, Thomas. 1967. *Christ the Tiger*. New York: J. B. Lippincott & Co.

———. 1969. *An Antique Drum*. New York: J. B. Lippincott & Co.

———. 1976. *Splendor in the Ordinary*. Wheaton, IL: Tyndale.

Irving, John. 2002. *A Prayer for Owen Mean*. New York: Modern Library.

Lakhani, Dave. 2005. *Persuasion: The Art of Getting What You Want*. Hoboken, NJ: John Wiley & Sons.

Lamott, Anne. 1994. *Bird by Bird*. New York: Anchor Books.

Lear, Jonathan. 1990. *Love and Its Place in Nature*. New York: Farrar, Straus and Giroux.

Lewis, C. S. 1940. *The Problem of Pain*. London: Collins.

———. 1943. *Mere Christianity*. New York: MacMillan Publishing.

———. 1946. *The Great Divorce*. New York: MacMillan Publishing.

———. 1955 *Surprised by Joy*. London: HarperCollins.

Lloyd-Jones, David Martyn. 1965. *Spiritual Depression: Its Causes and Cure.* Grand Rapids, MI: William B. Eerdmans.

Martel, Yanni. 2001. *Life of Pi.* New York: Harcourt.

National Council of Churches of the USA, Division of Christian Education. 1971. *Harper Study Bible: The Holy Bible, RSV.* Grand Rapids, MI: Zondervan Corporation.

Neuhaus, Richard John. 2000. *Death on a Friday Afternoon.* New York: Basic Books.

Peck, M. Scott. 1978. *The Road Less Traveled.* New York: Simon & Schuster.

Phillips, Michael. 1970. *The Seven Laws of Money.* New York: Random House.

Pittman, Frank. 1987. *Turning Points.* New York. W. W. Norton.

Remnick, David. 2000. Cornerman. *The New Yorker.* August 21 & 28

Schnarch, David. 1991. *Constructing the Sexual Crucible.* New York: W. W. Norton.

Sheed, Wilfred. 1995. *In Love with Daylight.* New York: Simon & Schuster.

Sulivan, Jean. 1976. *Morning Light.* New York: Paulist Press.

Taylor, Barbara Brown. 2006. *Leaving Church: A Memoir of Faith.* San Francisco: HarperCollins.

Wheelis, Allen. 1967. *The Doctor of Desire.* New York: W. W. Norton & Co.

———. 1973. *How People Change.* New York: Harper & Row.

Winget, Larry. 2004. *Shut Up, Stop Whining & Get a Life: A Kick-Butt Approach to a Better Life.* New York: John Wiley & Sons.

Updike, John. 1989. *Self-Consciousness.* New York: Alfred A. Knopf.

978-0-595-41792-6
0-595-41792-2

Printed in the United States
200303BV00005B/331-384/A